World War 2 for Teens

Major Battles of WWII, Turning Points, and Real-Life War Stories

Nick Weaver

TABLE OF CONTENTS

INTRODUCTION

In war, whichever side may call itself the victor, there are no winners, but all are losers.
–Neville Chamberlain

THESE WISE WORDS WERE SPOKEN BY THE FORMER PRIME Minister of Great Britain, Neville Chamberlain. All war is a catastrophe and leads to destructive outcomes, even for those who declare themselves victorious. This was certainly the case with World War Two which proved to be the deadliest conflict to ever occur on the face of the earth. From 1939 to 1945, the entire world was engulfed in a level of brutality never before witnessed in human history. Not only was there a conflict between nations and active battles between troops, but the scale of ethnic genocide aimed at Jewish individuals and other groups was momentous. The sheer size of the conflict made it a unique and unsurpassed period that continues to affect us to this very day.

In spite of this, World War Two provides us with many lessons on what we should not do in the future. You might have heard "never again" in history class when discussing this topic. But only stating this

1

is not enough. We must do all we can to learn about the tragedies that took place during the war. When reading about the features of the conflict, we should watch out for thinking only in terms of countries, ideologies, and statistics. Being informed about these facts certainly holds merit. Yet, we should remember that the war was filled with ordinary people with ambitions, goals, and dreams. Many of their lives were cut short through no fault of their own, and it is all these people that we should respect and learn from. Their lives are examples of what can happen if a dangerous person like Adolf Hitler sits at the helm.

This book is your guide to World War Two. It will teach you everything you want to know about the war by discussing major battles, turning points, and the Holocaust, to name only three. More importantly, it is filled with real-life war stories of teenagers and young people who actually witnessed and experienced certain wartime events that shaped the period. You will also be informed about aspects such as heroic leaders, why the war started in the first place, what happened when the conflict stopped, and even learn some bizarre facts that will definitely surprise you!

The book is structured so that you can read any chapter on its own that piques your interest. Still, it is recommended that you read it from the beginning, as some chapters include information referred to in previous ones. At the end of every chapter, you will find a personal story about someone who lived through the events discussed, which is followed by key takeaways so that you can recap what you learned while reading. As you read this book, you will find that teenagers played a big part in World War Two. They were put in concentration camps, some fought in battles, and others even played a part in turning the tide against the Axis powers! These individuals are a testament to the fact that you are never too young to do your part in making positive change.

Knowledge is power, and by learning the lessons that history provides, we can all ensure a brighter future. So, let's get to it. Go to Chapter One and start learning about World War Two!

CHAPTER 1:

The Beginnings of International Conflict

WAR HAS BEEN A REALITY SINCE THE BEGINNING OF TIME. how many times have you heard of a particular war on the news? What wars have you learned about in school? Unfortunately, the human race is one in which war remains a constant threat. Empires have fallen, communities have been wiped out, and the leadership structures of almost every country have changed several times due to international or civil conflict.

Some of these wars stand out, not only because they led to wide-scale death and destruction but because they changed the course of history. Two of the most catastrophic wars to ever take place occurred in the 20th century. The whole world was swept up in the Great War (also known as WWI) from 1914 to 1918, only to experience another one two decades later. World War Two—which lasted from 1939 to 1945—was the deadliest conflict to ever befall the globe. Our duty as future leaders is to learn all we can about the war to ensure that it never happens again. But first, let's look at four broad reasons why most wars usually happen in the first place.

The first common cause of war is economic or territorial gain. Whenever a country thinks that a region or group of resources belongs to them, they are more likely to invade in order to take control of it. An example of this was the Mexican–American War in the 1840s after America annexed Texas and the Mexicans fought back.

The second reason countries go to war is nationalism and ideological divides. Nationalism refers to an ideology that proposes that one's nation is the best and that one's allegiance to it is more important than anything else. Sometimes, different groups of people disagree when it comes to government policies or hold beliefs that are vastly different from mainstream thought. When separate groups disagree vehemently, conflict can arise. For instance, the American Civil War in the 1860s was fought between the South and the North because the former did not want to end slavery. Hence, they supported different ideologies and felt pride in what they believed their nation should promote.

The third cause is the conviction of a particular religion. This is similar to ideological divides, but in this case, conflict erupts as a result of a strongly held belief that one follows the "correct" religion and those who ascribe to a different one are in the wrong. An example of this was the constant conflict between Muslims and Hindus that ultimately led to the creation of an Islamic nation, Pakistan, right above Hindu-majority India.

The last reason is revenge on a nation or group that has seemingly done an entity wrong. Typically, these wars have deep-seated roots, and revenge-seeking is an additional factor. Revenge was part of the reason for the invasion of Afghanistan after terrorist attacks on the World Trade Center in New York on September 11, 2001. Afghanistan was believed to harbor many terrorists, and America wanted to punish them for the harm they inflicted at home.

The causes of World War Two were multifaceted, and one can find elements of all these reasons in explaining its outbreak. Several particular causes are generally thought to have been large contributors. One was the Treaty of Versailles. When Germany and its allies lost World War One, they were required to take the blame for having started the war. Upon signing the treaty, Germany was forced to disarm their military, pay former enemies' reparations, give up some European territories, and give up all of their colonies overseas. This brought great shame to the German people, who strongly felt that their nation was treated unfairly. Another cause was a bad economy. This was mainly due to the countless reparations the German government was forced to pay that consequently made them dependent on short-term loans from America. When the Great Depression struck in 1929, these loans were recalled, and Germany suffered high unemployment rates and hyperinflation that made the German currency, the reichsmark, practically meaningless. In fact, the year before the Nazis came to power, the unemployment rate was a staggering 29.9% (Gayle, 2018). Mass unhappiness and economic difficulties made German citizens more susceptible to nationalistic ideologies that might carry a solution. Some felt that a different political system would save their country from further decline, and the stage was set for an "us versus them" sentiment to enter mainstream thought. This opened the door for Nazism, a further cause of the war. Nazi ideologies became increasingly popular because they stressed the need for Germany to remain "pure" and to grow stronger in an international landscape that supposedly threatened their continued existence. Not only did the Nazis promise economic prosperity and national pride, but they promoted the idea of *Lebensraum*, a belief that Germany should expand its territory to unite all Germans and so spread their influence around the world. The last cause was widespread anti-Semitism, a term that refers to hostility toward the Jewish community. There existed strong prejudice against Jews for much of European history, and it was an integral part of the Nazi ideology. The Nazis viewed Jews and other minorities as inferior "races" that endangered the survival of ethnic or—what the Nazis called—Aryan Germans. Therefore, revenge, economic and territorial gains, nationalism, and ideological divides, were all involved in creating the atmosphere for World War Two to commence.

Who Was Adolf Hitler?

All these reasons were most strongly felt by one man who changed Germany forever. His name was Adolf Hitler. Today, World War Two is almost never mentioned without including his name in the conversation. Hitler was the chief instigator of the war, and without his leadership, it can be argued that the millions who lost their lives would not have died. It is, therefore, important to look at the life of the man who is believed by many to be the evilest person in history. By knowing who he was, what his beliefs were, and what drove him to war, one can have a greater understanding of the conflict. Before Hitler became chancellor of Germany in 1933, he had a rather humble childhood and a treacherous road to power. He was born in Austria on April 20, 1889, to Alois and Klara Hitler. Klara was much younger than Alois and suffered abuse from her husband, who also regularly beat Adolf and his siblings. At school, Adolf was described as a confident and outgoing boy. However, when his brother Edmund died in 1900, Adolf became more detached and introverted, opting to re-enact war battles in his free time. Alois was a customs official and wanted his son to become a civil servant, often putting tremendous pressure on young Adolf concerning his schoolwork. When Alois died suddenly in 1903,

Adolf's academics deteriorated, and his soft-spoken mother allowed him to leave school when he was 16. Adolf had no career plans but had a passion for art and applied to study at the Vienna Academy of Fine Arts. Unfortunately, he was rejected twice.

These rejections did not seem to stop him from trying to find a purpose in Vienna, and he did not return to his native Linz. Klara died of breast cancer when Adolf was only 18, and he found himself truly lost. He squandered away his inheritance from his parents and dismissed calls from extended family, urging him to follow in his father's professional footsteps. Adolf showed no desire for this and opted to stay in homeless shelters and men's dormitories. He sustained himself by selling his paintings and postcards and, at times, as a general laborer. This difficult period in Vienna was also the start of his interest in far-right politics. He despised the cosmopolitan and multinational nature of Vienna and started delving into nationalist and racist philosophies. Anti-Semitism was also rife in the region, and the impressionable Adolf soon became a radical supporter of this prejudiced notion. He came to believe that the German-speaking world was superior to all others, and he despised European leaders who supported diversity. In 1913, he moved to Munich, Germany, and this is where he was at the outbreak of World War One. He petitioned to serve in the German Army and found his true passion: warfare. Adolf was such an effective soldier that he was awarded two decorations for bravery but was required to leave the battlefield after a gas attack left him partially blind in 1918. It was in the hospital that he first learned of the German surrender and the disgrace that the new government—the Weimar Republic—brought to the German people upon signing the Treaty of Versailles. He quickly returned to Munich with a strong love of war and a rabid obsession with German nationalism.

Portrait of Adolf Hitler, 1930's

Once there, he found a home in a small political party called the German Workers Party. Adolf was intrigued with the ideologies of the party and rose through the ranks of leadership. By 1920, he was in charge of the party's propaganda and was instrumental in changing its name to the National Socialist German Party or Nazi Party. In 1921, he so impressed party members with his oratory skills that he became its leader. His speeches were effective, and many former army officers were recruited into the party. The inclusion of talented military men emboldened Hitler to stage a revolution that would remove the Weimar Republic and give all power to the Nazis. On November 8, 1923, the Nazis attempted this in what became known as the Beer Hall Putsch. They were unsuccessful, and Adolf was sent to prison. Yet before he was incarcerated, his trial was followed by many Germans who began to like the "impressive" speaker. Simply put, the trial gave him a voice and a wider audience. While in prison, Adolf wrote *Mein Kampf*, which is German for "my struggle." In the book, he offered plans for Germany's future, and it ultimately became a manifesto on what the entire Nazi ideology stood for. It was in this book that his racist tendencies were first recorded, and he used his time in prison to strategize on how he would make this book a reality. When he was released, he got to work structuring the Nazi Party into a formal political party and how their message would be promoted. At first, the Nazis were not successful in elections, but in 1932 they got 38% of the vote (Childers, 2021). They were now relatively powerful in government and used the lack of unity and chaos among the opposition to further consolidate their power. In January of the next year, German President Paul von Hindenburg appointed Adolf Hitler as chancellor, and in March 1933, the parliament building suspiciously burnt down, a situation that Hitler used to pass the Enabling Act that dissolved all other political parties. The Nazis were now all-powerful, with Hitler as their leader. The Third Reich had finally begun.

Hitler speaks at Party Rally – the slogan reads "Give Adolf Hitler Strength! Vote National Socialism!", 1930's

Once in power, Hitler immediately began implementing the policies he promoted in his book. In order to do this properly, he concluded that his political enemies should be removed so as not to threaten the autocratic power he intended to hold until he died. During the Night of Long Knives on June 29, 1934, hundreds of people were murdered by the Schutzstaffel (SS), a group of Nazi soldiers who swore a personal oath to Hitler. With no pushback, he soon enacted racist policies in an attempt to rid Germany of its Jewish population. Every aspect of society was changed, with Nazi propaganda constantly spread across the media. In time, a cult of personality around Hitler started to take form, with many Germans believing Hitler to be a savior of sorts. Every citizen was expected to worship him and greet each other with the Nazi salute in professional settings. If anyone spoke out against him or the party, they were imprisoned or executed, and there was no freedom of speech or thought in any segment of society. Hitler had the trust of many Germans and used his six years in power to ready the nation for possible war as he expanded the nation's territory. A year before World War Two, Hitler ordered the annexation of Austria and the Czechoslovak Republic. These were promising as Germany suffered no pushback from the international community. Nonetheless, his actions signified a slow progression toward war, and in September 1939, it was all to erupt.

War Erupts!

On the morning of September 1, 1939, Poland was experiencing a beautiful, sunny day with clear, blue skies. This was all to change a few hours later when the Nazis marched in and brought darkness with them. Before Hitler ordered the invasion, he had strategized with military officials to ensure a successful annexation. They had decided on a tactic known as blitzkrieg, meaning "lightning War." As the name would suggest, the goal was to attack in a quick fashion and reach their objectives with minimal soldier and artillery losses. There were two main steps in this strategy. Firstly, the destruction of all communication lines, railroads, and the air force, would subsequently lead to chaos and the inability of the enemy to work on their defensive strategy. Once these elements have all been removed, the second step commenced: a land invasion. During the attack on Poland, Germany deployed 2,000 war tanks, 400 fighter planes, about 900 bombers, and 1.5 million soldiers (*Invasion of Poland*, 2019)! This vastly outnumbered the Polish forces, who lacked modern equipment and trained soldiers. Germany easily broke through Polish defenses and destroyed towns all over the country. Britain and France—who were both Polish allies—were concerned about Hitler's invasion and what it would mean for a safe and civilized Europe. They did not fall for Hitler's supposed reasoning that ethnic Germans were being persecuted in Poland. Neville Chamberlain, the Prime Minister of Britain, immediately sent an ultimatum to Hitler that he should leave or face war with his country and France. Of course, Hitler did not respond, and the two countries officially declared war on Germany on September 3. In a radio address to the nation, Chamberlain said, "For it is evil things that we shall be fighting against, brute force, bad faith, injustice, oppression, and persecution; and against them I am certain that the right will prevail" (Chamberlain, 2008). The French President, Albert Lebrun, also explained his reasoning behind going to war with Germany. He said, "They [French citizens] realize that over and above the fate of their own country, the freedom of the world, and the future of civilisation are both at stake" (Lebrun, 2008). World War Two had officially started.

German troops parade before Hitler in Warsaw after the invasion of Poland, 1939

Of course, other countries were to become enmeshed in the war, but at first, it was only Britain and France against Nazi Germany. To make matters worse, the Soviet Union had signed a nonaggression pact with Germany months prior that ensured that there would be no Soviet reaction when Hitler invaded Poland. In fact, two weeks after the invasion, the Soviets invaded the east of Poland, with the reasoning being that there were ethnic Russians behind the border who wanted to join the greater union. When the Germans surrounded the capital of Poland, Warsaw, the Polish government knew there was no point in fighting back. Heavy shelling and bombing had left their capital in disrepair, and they officially surrendered to the German and Soviet forces on September 28, 1939. One day later, the Germans and Soviets agreed on a demarcation of the country that drew a line along the Bug River. The Polish defensive units were disbanded, and all former citizens were forced to accept that their country was now dissolved. Hitler set up a satellite government under the leadership of Nazi Hans Frank and soon began to implement his racist policies there. Poles were at the mercy of Nazi rule, and many Jews and other minorities were murdered. However, Hitler was not finished. He was quick to strategize regarding his next steps that would finally bring the whole of Europe under his control. The fall of Poland instigated a lot of fear concerning the future of the continent around the world. Practically every country faced the question of whether they would support Hitler, support those who were against him, or stay out of the conflict altogether. In time, more countries were to join in the war effort, and a full-scale world war commenced. Hitler had planted the seed for international hostility and was ultimately responsible for the creation of the Allies and Axis powers, which resulted in tremendous death and destruction around the globe. The invasion of Poland was just the beginning.

The Story of Renia Spiegel

When reading up on the invasion of Poland, it is easy to view the circumstances from a birds-eye-view. In other words, one often forgets that every Polish person is unique and has a story to tell. Their treatment is often lost to history because many died during the conflict. Not so for Renia Spiegel, a Polish Jew who experienced the horrors of Nazi occupation first-hand. She kept a meticulous diary of her life during the war that was only found decades after her death. Stories like hers should be told so that we never forget the atrocities the average person—child or adult—had to endure. Renia was born in a small Polish town on June 18, 1924. She grew up with her mother, father, and little sister on her father's large estate. They were a happy family that did not struggle financially, and the children had big dreams for their future. In 1938, when Renia was just 14, her mother moved to Warsaw with her sister, who was a prominent child actress. Renia, on the other hand, was sent to her grandparent's home in the Polish town of Przemyśl. She was there during the Invasion of September 1939. At first, Renia was hopeful that her nation would be able to fend off the enemy, writing, "I'm fighting alongside the rest of the Polish nation; I'm fighting and we will win!" (Spiegel, 2018). Her hopeful spirit came crashing down on September 10. "My God! We've been on the road for three days now; Przemyśl was attacked, we had to flee" (Spiegel, 2018). Sadly, her grandmother stayed behind as she was unable to move as fast as the others. Renia stayed in the town of Lwow, constantly worrying about her parents and whether they were still alive in Warsaw. Unbeknownst to her, her mother survived. Renia was a religious girl who regularly wrote prayers in her diary. One entry on September 18 states, "Merciful God, please make the war stop, make all good and happy. Amen" (Spiegel, 2018). She was in Lwow when the Poles surrendered, and the Soviets took control of her region.

When the Poles stopped fighting back, Renia was relieved at first. She was able to go back to Soviet-controlled Przemyśl and continue her schooling there. She did not expect the conflict to ensue into a world war and was hoping that she could live her life as normally as possible. Her diary is full of everyday encounters, not that different from those experienced by teenagers today. In particular, while at school, she fell in love with a Jewish boy called Zygmunt Schwarzer, whom she lovingly called "Zygu." By all accounts, Renia was the happiest when she spent time with him. One diary entry about a party she accompanied him to reads, "What was the best moment? Was it when he spoke to me while we were dancing? Or when he draped his arm around me as I stumbled during the waltz? He smelled so amazing!" (Spiegel, 2018). Their love grew, and Renia felt extremely hurt when another girl, Irka, invited him to a different party! Renia was the picture of an infatuated teenager and concerned herself with everything an adolescent girl would usually be focused on. Sadly, once Germany declared war on the Soviet Union, the former moved in on her town, and it fell under Nazi rule. She, and all other Jews, were required to wear the yellow star, abandon school, and follow all the anti-Semitic policies dictated by Hitler. She wrote about the mass killings of people she knew and was devastated when she was forced to move into a Jewish ghetto, writing, "We feared it, and then it finally happened: the ghetto" (Spiegel, 2018). Adding, "My soul is very sad; my heart is seized with terror" (Spiegel, 2018). She endured hunger, death, and loneliness. When it became clear that Jews were being rounded up to go to concentration camps, Schwarzer—who was part of the resistance—sneaked Renia out and housed her in the attic of his uncle's house. Her last diary entry is dated July 25, 1942, when she was just 18 years old. "O, Israel, save us, help us; God, into Your hands I commit myself (Spiegel, 2018). Five days after this entry, the Nazis found Renia and ruthlessly dragged her out into the street. She stood with Schwarzer's parents as they were all executed by Nazi police. A tragic end to a short, memorable life. Renia is only one of the millions of teenagers who were killed by the Nazis. When we learn about these stories, we are able to appreciate the lives we have been given. We should never let stories like that of Renia Spiegel be forgotten!

Key Takeaways

- There are four broad reasons that underlie most wars. They are economic and territorial gain, nationalism and ideological divides, the conviction of a certain religion, and revenge.

- The causes of World War Two are complex but can generally fall within four umbrella notions. Namely, the Treaty of Versailles, an economic downturn, Nazism and Lebensraum, and anti-Semitism.

- Adolf Hitler was the Chancellor of Germany from 1933 and instigated the war with goals of territorial expansion and extermination of "non-Aryan" peoples.

- World War Two officially broke out on September 1, 1939, when Germany invaded Western Poland. In response, Britain and France declared war on Germany. Two weeks later, the Soviet Union invaded Eastern Poland and annexed a significant portion of the country.

CHAPTER 2:

The Reality of WWII

"OLDER MEN DECLARE WAR. BUT IT IS THE YOUTH THAT must die; and it is the youth who must inherit the tribulation, the sorrow, and the triumphs that are the aftermath of the war" (Case, 2013, p. 203). Former American President Herbert Hoover spoke these words in 1944 as the war in Europe was raging. His sentiment has been true for most wars, and particularly World War Two. In fact, the average age of a combat soldier in the war was 26, whereas the leaders of involved nations were predominantly over the age of 50! As these older men strategized in secure war rooms, their young countrymen were dying at a rapid pace. Every one of these soldiers had a family and loved ones, undoubtedly praying for their safe return. Sadly, about 15,000,000 did not return and were only remembered for the ultimate sacrifice they made for their nation. It was not only soldiers who lost their lives. 45,000,000 civilians also died—in active conflict, through mass murder, and from diseases directly related to the conditions that a war scenario creates. Throughout the war, these soldiers fought for either the Axis or Allied alliances. The reasoning behind each country throwing its hat in the ring with either was vastly different, and their involvement was heavily linked to their own national security. Some nations even entered the war unwillingly, such as South Africa. They were technically forced to join the Allies due to their status as a dominion of the British Empire. Three countries soon took the lead in each of these power structures, and by looking at their involvement, the greater one can understand the reality of World War Two. Let's delve into the Axis and Allied powers that spearheaded six years of international conflict.

The Axis Powers

In simple terms, the Axis powers were the aggressors of the war. They were the countries that were viewed as having started the conflict and continued its brutality. Their goals were related to that of Hitler, such as territorial expansion and greater influence in their regions. Three main countries formed this alliance: Germany, Italy, and Japan. The reasoning for Germany's instigation of the war was already discussed in Chapter One. Namely, Hitler wanted to increase German influence in Europe and the world. At this stage, it is helpful to mention the branches of the military that he used to try and reach these objectives. The Nazi military had several subdivisions that generally fell under one of three commands. Firstly, they boasted the *Heer*, or army, that traveled on foot and were involved in actual bodily conflict. Secondly, the *Luftwaffe*, or air force, was responsible for bombing enemy territory and gaining air superiority by wiping out enemy aircraft. Thirdly, the *Kriegsmarine*, or navy, fought on the water by attacking enemy ships and using submarines to bomb vessels before they had the chance to make landfall. Germany suffered significant losses during the war, with some estimates pointing to about 5,300,000 deaths on the battlefield. Most of Germany's offensives began on the Western Front and later the

Eastern Front. As the Allied Forces turned the tide in their favor, both these Fronts required the Germans to go on the defensive so as to maintain the territories they had already annexed.

You might be wondering why any country would want to align itself with Hitler's evil regime. However, it is more complicated than that. Italy sided with Germany for several reasons. Perhaps the most candid reason was that Italy was an autocratic state under the leadership of Benito Mussolini. The running of his government was closely aligned with the political system promoted by the Nazis. Additionally, Italy was threatened by the growing influence of Western European countries—like Britain and France—that were prosperous and functioning democracies. Throughout the 1930s, Italy saw Nazi Germany as an ally due to their political similarities, which eventually culminated in both countries signing the Pact of Steel in 1939. This agreement was a promise that they would protect each other if either was attacked by foreign entities that threatened their ideologies. Italy also had territorial ambitions in parts of Turkey and Northern Africa that they believed Germany could help them with, given the latter's superior military capacity. Any attack on Germany was therefore viewed as an attack on Italy's interests, and they were required by the pact to uphold this relationship and assist in their war efforts. As World War Two continued, the Allied powers naturally fought with Italy, as there was no difference between their ambitions and Nazi goals. During the conflict, Italy lost about 301,000 soldiers on the battlefield—this number did not include the innumerable civilian deaths when Allied forces attacked Italian cities and towns.

Adolf Hitler and Benito Mussolini in Munich, Germany, 1940

The last country to join the Axis powers in 1940 was Japan. After they got involved in the war, the three countries became known as the Tripartite Alliance. Many are confused as to why an island in the far east would willingly take part in a European conflict on the side of Hitler! As with Italy, Japan was largely autocratic under Emperor Hirohito. The difference in ideologies with the Western world made Germany and Italy friendlier toward them as opposed to other liberal and democratic countries. Moreover, Japan is a relatively small island, and Emperor Hirohito yearned for more territory in lands in and around the Pacific Ocean. At the time, the United States and Great Britain had enormous influence in the Pacific, which made Japan a natural enemy. Japanese leaders thought that Germany and Italy's interests were closely aligned with theirs, and after the three countries signed the Tripartite Pact, Japan was obliged to fight the powers opposed to Axis ideals. Although Japan is far from Europe, it suffered significantly during the war. An estimated 2,120,000 Japanese soldiers died, and their two cities of Hiroshima and Nagasaki were decimated after the United States dropped two atomic bombs in 1945. Several other countries joined the Axis powers, such as Bulgaria and Romania, who feared Soviet expansion into their regions. But the three tripartite nations headed the majority of the conflict.

The Allied Powers

The Allied powers were those countries that formed the defensive component. This means that they entered the war in order to stop Germany from winning. That being said, as the war came to a close, the Allied powers went on the offensive to retrieve territories captured by the Axis powers. Many nations formed part of this group, but three of them stood out: Great Britain, the United States, and the Soviet Union. During the first half of the 20th century, Britain was far more influential than it is today. At the time war broke out, Britain controlled many areas of the world and was a dominant cultural force. This is why they were the first to declare war after the Polish invasion. Britain was a democracy and did not want the hateful ideology of Nazism to engulf the European continent. If Germany was to gain more territories and win, the balance of power would completely change, and Britain would suffer in immeasurable ways. The prime minister of Britain certainly did not want to go to war a mere two decades after his nation suffered through World War One, but he believed it necessary to become the protector of Europe and gather allies to defeat the Axis powers. Britain is remembered as having been incredibly strong in their response to German attacks and was one of only a few nations that never saw a direct land attack on the homeland, although it suffered from countless bombing missions from the powerful Luftwaffe. About 383,000 British soldiers were killed on the battlefield, but these numbers are skewed.

Nations under British control, such as South Africa and Australia, lost 11,900 and 39,000 soldiers, respectively. Hence the number of "British" casualties is far larger than usually stated.

Like Britain, the United States did not want to enter the war. They remembered the suffering of World War One and tried their best to support Britain from a safe distance. This all changed when Japan attacked the American naval base in Pearl Harbor, Hawaii, on December 7, 1941. The reasoning behind the ambush was so that Japan could eradicate the American fleet and buy themselves time as they annexed territories in the Pacific around Hawaii. During the unprovoked assault, 2,403 American sailors died, and many navy ships were damaged or destroyed. Americans knew that they could no longer sit back as they were now a direct target. In response, the American government declared war on Japan and, in doing so, indirectly declared war on all the Axis powers. From this perspective, it can be argued that the United States was sucked into a war they did not think deserved their manpower and weapons. But once their own territory was attacked, they realized that it was time to become an active member of the Allied powers. In a short time, they not only sent soldiers to Japanese battlefields but sent their men to the Western and Eastern Fronts in Europe. America became instrumental in arranging dialogue between Allied leaders and organized military strategies so effectively that some historians believe the U.S. involvement turned the tide against Hitler. Sadly, their support came at a heavy cost. About 416,800 American soldiers died on the battlefield in the name of liberty and freedom, two pillars on which their nation rested.

Japanese attack on Pearl Harbor, Hawaii, 1941

The Soviet Union was perhaps most unenthusiastic about entering the war on the side of the Allied powers. The country was in the midst of economic development and other national ventures. In fact, they welcomed the Polish invasion because it gave them a chance to take a piece of that country! At first, Soviet leadership trusted in the pact their nation had made with Germany in 1939 that supposedly ensured that they wouldn't be attacked. Of course, Hitler did not follow through on this agreement. In June 1941, Germany attacked the Soviet Union, with Hitler believing the country would fall quickly. The Nazis misjudged the courage and unity of the Russian people due to the Soviet Union being a relatively young communist country. Russian soldiers and civilians fought back with passion, and the Eastern Front—a line on the edge of the Soviet Union—became the most brutal front in the entire war. Russians were not pleased that they had to ally themselves with countries like Britain and America, who were strongly opposed to their political ideology, but recognized that it was necessary in order to protect their own nation. As the old saying goes, "The enemy of my enemy is my friend." It was the decision to invade the Soviet Union that started to show cracks in the might of the German military. Fighting with the Soviets proved to be the most devastating when looking at their number of casualties. An estimated 10,700,000 Russian soldiers and countless civilians lost their lives. Even so, the aftermath of the war created great tension between the Soviet Union and the United States that culminated in the Cold War; more on that later!

Military Developments

Both powers used new and innovative technologies never before seen in warfare. The early 20th century saw many technological developments that naturally influenced military equipment and weapons. Unfortunately, technological advancements are responsible for World War Two being much more vicious and deadly than World War One. When looking at a few of these innovations, it becomes clear why so many people lost their lives on the battlefield. Let's look at new equipment on the ground first. Although both world wars used trenches and primitive weapons like knives to reach their objectives, the introduction of modern tanks upped the game. World War Two tanks were faster, more mechanically robust, and highly reliable vehicles that enabled Hitler's Blitzkrieg strategy to thrive. The "Tiger tank" was used by the feared Panzer divisions in the German *Heer*. In response, the Allied powers developed their own versions that were just as efficient, such as the American Sherman tank and the Soviet T-34 tanks. With regard to ocean travel, the war introduced the world to aircraft carriers. These are large ships that serve as mobile airports of sorts. Before their invention, airplanes needed to stay close to land in order to refuel. After aircraft carriers came onto the scene, it was possible to launch an air attack from anywhere in the world.

British Sherman Tank, the Firefly at the Battle of the Bulge, 1944

Speaking of air attacks, World War Two was the breeding ground for modern air combat. The first military helicopters were designed and used during the conflict, as well as the first jet-powered fighter planes. It was also the first time that planes were specifically designed for a single purpose. Small fighter planes were used for air-to-air combat, transport planes were used to deliver soldiers and supplies to a certain region, and large bombers were used to drop bombs on the enemy. To make things easier for pilots, the new technology of radar was developed and employed by Britain so that navigation was easier and enemies could be spotted by a dot on a radar screen. No longer did pilots have to wait and see the enemy with their own eyes! Different bombs were also developed so that they could meet certain objectives.

For example, the Germans used long-range and rocket bombs, whereas the Allied powers used a special bomb that bounced on the water until it reached its target. One of the most damaging bombs also produced during this period was the atomic bomb. The introduction of nuclear weapons was—and continues to be—controversial due to their capacity for causing death and destruction on a massive scale, as evidenced by the atomic bombs dropped on Hiroshima and Nagasaki, to be discussed later.

German Luftwaffe, Heinkel He 111 bombers during the Battle of Britain, 1940

In the area of communication, the war also broke barriers. Both sides implemented secret codes that could be understood by their war partners but made no sense to the enemy. The Germans developed the Enigma machine that was able to code and decode information sent between military commanders, soldiers, and the Axis powers. Yet this did not outsmart the Allied powers, who employed scientists to crack the code later on. The last component was not designed for the purpose of war but gave rise to a new way in which it was managed. When World War Two started, communicative instruments like radios, microphones, and motion pictures were widely used, and both powers used these to their advantage. They were employed as modes of propaganda that riled up support for their respective war efforts. In fact, Nazi Germany had a government agency known as the Reich Ministry of Public Enlightenment and Propaganda, run by the notorious Joseph Goebbels. He organized radio broadcasts, speeches, and pro-Nazi films to enter society and so get public support. The Allied powers also used these instruments to their advantage. For instance, from 1941 to 1945, the American government and Disney collaborated to produce anti-Nazi films. In one of these, Donald Duck is even situated in Nazi Germany! Therefore, World War Two was one of many firsts and completely changed the mainstream understanding of war.

The Story of Stan Scott

Many teenagers fought in the war for both the Axis and Allied powers. One of these was the native Brit Stan Scott. He was still in school when the war broke out and was particularly affected after the Battle of Britain damaged the country he was so proud of. In 1941—at the age of 15—Stan was so emboldened that he went to the authorities to enlist in the army. The British military was overly enthusiastic about getting more men to serve their country and failed to look at Stan's age. In order to get in, the boy lied and told them he was 18. Naturally, his mother became concerned when her son did not return home. At first, she explained it away as him visiting friends or family, but as time went on, she grew very worried about her son's whereabouts. She had heard that he might have enlisted and contacted the authorities to check whether they had her son. It was only then that they became aware of his age and sent him home. You can imagine the argument he had with his mother that evening! However, Stan was not finished. Only a year later, he enlisted again and, due to his age, was now allowed to do a "menial" job in the army. He was tasked with guarding aerodromes in the town of Kent to warn other soldiers if the Germans were to attack from the sky. Unfortunately, he quickly grew bored of the inaction this job required and joined the British commandos right after he turned 18.

Now was his time to be part of the action. That same year, he was shipped off to Normandy, where he was an active participant in the D-Day invasion. He remembered, "[We] hit the beach, down went the ramps. Whack! Next thing I hear is someone saying, 'Get up, Scotty, you're not hurt'" (Mason, 2019). Stan saw many of his battle buddies die, and his own life was in danger when a bomb landed right next to him. Luckily, he survived and continued fighting relentlessly. You might think that seeing the destruction up close might have caused him to run the other way, but Stan once said, "I never thought I would break down—I was too streetwise" (Mason, 2019). During his service, he was involved in five European river crossings and was even captured by the Germans along with 75 other troop members. Out of the 75, only 19 survived, of which Stan was one. Toward the end of the war, he was instrumental in freeing the inmates of the Belsen concentration camp and helped many weakened survivors leave the facility. You can imagine the gratitude he felt for having survived all these scenarios, and he returned to Britain victorious. Throughout the rest of his life, he remained tremendously proud of British efforts in the war and served as the Chairman of the Commando Veterans Association until he died. His life came to an end on June 25, 2014, but he will always be remembered as a brave and fearless soldier who risked his life for his country. Stan's story proves that you are never too young to make a difference and do your part in turning the tide on injustice and hate. All we can say is, well done, Trooper Stan Scott!

Key Takeaways

- World War Two was the most brutal war ever, with an estimated loss of 15,000,000 soldiers and 45,000,000 civilians.

- The fighting happened between countries divided into two groups. The Axis powers and the Allied powers.

- The three main nations that formed the Axis powers were Germany, Italy, and Japan.

- The three main nations that formed the Allied powers were Great Britain, the United States, and the Soviet Union.

- The war saw many new technologies. These included more reliable military tanks, new aircraft, aircraft carriers, radar, stronger bombs, secret codes, and the use of "modern" technology to spread propaganda to the masses.

CHAPTER 3:

The Bloodiest Battles

WE SHALL FIGHT ON THE BEACHES, WE SHALL FIGHT ON the landing grounds, we shall fight in the fields and in the streets, we shall fight in the hills; we shall never surrender!" (Abbot, 2010, p. 180). This was said in a speech by Winston Churchill, the British prime minister who came to power in 1940. His sentiment was shared among all the national militaries of the Axis and Allied powers. This refusal to surrender—at any cost—made World War Two a conflict characterized by extreme brutality. No side wanted to lose, and they literally fought to death for victory. There were thousands of battles during the six years of conflict, yet some stand out due to various factors, such as the death toll and the impact they had in changing the trajectory of the war. Sadly, many soldiers and civilians were lost in battles that do not even have a name. Nevertheless, when you look at some of the larger, more influential battles, you will recognize that each shaped our current understanding of the war. For this reason, six of the bloodiest battles will be discussed by looking at the various elements that made them so important. Our first stop: the Battle of Dunkirk.

The Battle of Dunkirk

Many misunderstand the Battle of Dunkirk because it was not an active battle at first. It all started on May 10, 1940, when Hitler ordered the German forces to expand further into Western Europe. British troops had been stationed on the French border by the North Sea since Britain and France declared war in September the previous year. The British soldiers there were not actively involved in battle because their role was seen more as a protective measure to protect their ally, France. However, as May progressed, Germany was moving closer to them by annexing Holland and Belgium. Upon seeing the rapid successes of the German army, Britain and France began to worry. Blitzkrieg was proving to be wildly effective, and the thousands of British forces in France faced the possibility of being cut off and destroyed. Additionally, their military equipment was inferior to the Germans, and Britain could not afford to lose so many soldiers before having time to prepare. Churchill, the British prime minister, immediately started working on ways in which his soldiers could be evacuated from the region. His officials suggested that they evacuate the men through the beach of a French town called Dunkirk.

Soldiers from the British Expeditionary Force fire at low flying German aircraft during the Dunkirk evacuation, 1940

The evacuation became known as Operation Dynamo and subsequently became the most successful of its kind in history. Between May 26 and June 4, 338,000 British and allied troops were rescued from Dunkirk by British and French warships, as well as civilian boats (Holland, 2020). In fact, many pleasure cruisers and private fishing boats even transported some soldiers!

The evacuation of the British troops. Dunkirk, 1940

Surprisingly, as the evacuation was ongoing, Hitler ordered a halt order of 48 hours that restricted German forces from advancing toward Dunkirk. No clear reason for this was given, but one can suspect that he did not want a direct battle with Britain just yet. The success of Operation Dynamo was mainly due to the orderly manner in which it was implemented. One of the evacuees, Alfred Baldwin, remembered, "You had the impression of people standing waiting for a bus; there was no pushing or shoving" (Slater, 2018). The Allies also left and disabled their military equipment so that the German army could not use it in the future. When the British soldiers returned home, it was a great morale boost for the nation. Accomplishing such a task meant that they could do anything if they remained calm and unified. Sadly, many allied troops—especially the French—stayed behind and were forced to battle the Germans when they finally made landfall at Dunkirk. About 22,000 Allied troops lost their lives, as did 2,000 civilians and 20,000 German troops (Woerner, 2021). Similarly, after many Allied forces left, Germany had less pushback.

British soldiers from France arrive in southern England aboard a destroyer, 1940

The Battle of France

The Battle of France was a German victory that emboldened Hitler to broaden his quest for European expansion. This battle technically began on May 10, 1940, during the same time the Battle of Dunkirk was ongoing. It formed part of a widespread German invasion of Western Europe in an attempt to annex as many countries as they could. As was mentioned, Hitler annexed Holland and Belgium, in addition to the small nation of Luxembourg during this time. Before the outbreak of the war, France had built a line of fortifications—the Maginot Line—on their border with Germany but failed to build a strong one on their border with Belgium. Germany's annexation of Belgium was, therefore, strategic because it was an easier gateway into

France. After Hitler annexed these nations, he could focus solely on getting France under his control. Moreover, after British troops evacuated Dunkirk, he knew that France had inadequate Allied support to help them fend off German advances. Hitler ordered his troops to attack France by going through the lush Ardennes Forest in Belgium. This was highly unexpected as the French did not think that Germany would pass through such a difficult landscape. The majority of French troops were sent to a different region in Belgium, which unfortunately left the small number of troops in the Ardennes Forest incapable of resisting an invasion.

German tank with SS-Panzer-Division "Hitlerjugend" during the Battle of France, 1940

Days after the Dunkirk evacuation was completed, the German air force started bombing the French capital, Paris, on June 3, 1940. German troops successfully crossed the Maginot Line and the fronts built beside the Somme River. It became clear that Germany was going to take Paris. The French desperately asked Great Britain for assistance, but the latter did not want to send their troops in case Germany attacked their nation in the future. The French troops did their best to keep the Germans out of Paris, but as the conflict continued, about half of the French army was either killed or captured.

Chaos on the streets of Macon during the Battle of France, 1940

A mere 10 days after the Germans first crossed the French lines of defense, they captured Paris on June 22. French authorities knew that there was no point in fighting back and signed an armistice agreement that same day. Hitler wanted revenge for Germany's humiliation concerning the Treaty of Versailles and insisted the French sign the armistice on the same train on which the treaty was signed more than two decades ago. The day after Germany annexed France, Hitler triumphantly rode through the streets of Paris, indulging in their victory. During the conflict, an estimated 90,000 French were killed, an estimated 200,000 suffered severe wounds, and 1,800,000 were taken prisoner by Germany (*Battle of France*, 2007).

Hitler giving the Nazi salute from his Mercedes-Benz in Berlin after his visit to German-occupied Paris, 1940

The Battle of Midway

The Battle of Midway was a landmark moment during World War Two as it resulted in Japan losing a lot of influence in the Pacific. The importance of this battle is even more fascinating when you realize that it was fought in only four days! Although the battle started in June 1942, the cause of its breaking out is actually attributed to something that happened two months earlier. On April 18, 1942, America attacked islands that were the property of Japan; in what was known as the Doolittle Raid. Of course, this angered the Japanese, who wanted to make the United States pay for encroaching on their territory. Because Pearl Harbor was unsuccessful and did not break American morale, the Japanese were further emboldened to finally get the job done. They figured that their best chance to push the Americans out of the Pacific was to ambush the American army base on the island of Midway. Midway was in a strategic location and would help Japan tremendously in realizing its war objectives. Japan planned to sneakily attack the island, catching the United States off guard. It was hoped that they would destroy American aircraft carriers as they rested in the dock. However, American cryptanalysts were hard at work and soon deciphered Japanese transmissions. Unbeknownst to Japan, the United States knew exactly what they were planning.

Devastators on the USS Enterprise in Battle of Midway, 1942

Ironically, the Japanese attack was led by Admiral Yamamoto, the same man who planned the attacks on Pearl Harbor. On June 4, they put their plan into action and traveled to Midway with four aircraft carriers and many fighter planes. As they approached the island, the Americans surprised them by waiting on the path toward Midway. Japan did not expect them to be there, and their carriers were hit with countless bombs from American fighter planes. At first, they did not hit any of the ships. But when dive bombers attacked from higher in the sky, three of the Japanese vessels were sunk in succession. One of the most ferocious incidents occurred between the American carrier, Yorktown, and the Japanese carrier, the Hiryu. Both vessels launched bombers to attack the other, and both sank with a great loss of life. On June 7, Japan lost all the aircraft carriers they sent to Midway. It was a major turning point in the Pacific because Japan lost four of its most efficient weapons of war. Additionally, they lost 248 aircraft and more than 3,000 soldiers (*Battle of Midway*, 2019). America was, therefore, victorious and continued operating from Midway as a military base. The Japanese were humiliated, and many citizens began to question their country's involvement in the worldwide conflict.

Japanese cruiser Mikuma shortly before sinking during Battle of Midway, 1942

The Battle of Stalingrad

The Battle of Stalingrad was one of the deadliest conflicts in the war. In order to make sense of this battle, you need to know where the city of Stalingrad was situated and why it was important to the Soviet Union. The city was found near the western border of the Soviet Union. During this time, the Soviet Union was rapidly increasing its industrial ventures and consolidating its new political ideology of communism. Their leader, Josef Stalin, held Stalingrad in high esteem, and the Russian people renamed the city in honor of him. Hitler had long had his eyes on the country due to the sheer mass of land it inhabited and what occupation would mean for the expansion of Nazi ideologies. Additionally, Hitler thought that if he was to invade the region, the relatively new communist state would fall, and he could take over in a quick manner. On June 22, 1941, Hitler ordered his soldiers to break the nonaggression pact and invade the Soviet Union from the West. At first, they were successful and got very close to the capital city, Moscow. However, the Russians fought back, and the Germans were forced to retreat. Yet, Hitler was not finished.

Nazi German machine gunner in Stalingrad, 1942

In late-1942, he spearheaded the invasion of Stalingrad. The Germans used their Blitzkrieg strategy and first bombed the Volga River and, thereafter, the city, resulting in Stalingrad being reduced to rubble. The German army then moved in and was able to take a large part of the region. Citizens and soldiers alike fought back by launching surprise attacks. Some even hid in the sewers and waited for approaching Germans before they jumped out and ambushed them! The weather was very cold, and most Germans soldiers were not used to the treacherous temperatures. Hence, not only did they suffer from surprise attacks, but intense weather conditions as well. In November, the Soviets planned a counterattack and put it into effect just as the Germans started losing morale. The Russians surrounded the city and practically trapped the soldiers from leaving. In time, Germans were starving to death and dying of hypothermia. On February 2, the next year, Nazi General Friedrich Paulus surrendered. Hitler was beside himself with rage as he fully expected to be victorious. The Germans were subsequently run out of the Soviet Union, and no Russian territory was ever in their hands. During the months of conflict, it is estimated that 750,000 Germans and about 500,000 Russians tragically died (*Battle of Stalingrad*, 2019). Today, the brave Russians who fought back are celebrated across the nation by marking the anniversary of their victory day. In 2018, Russian President Vladimir Putin said that the Battle of Stalingrad "opened the path to the complete destruction of the enemy" (RFE, 2018).

Red Army, Stalingrad, 1942

The Battle of Bulge

The Battle of Bulge stands out because it was the last attempt by Germany to push the Allies out of Europe. After Germany was defeated, most of their successive battles were more defensive. The battle officially began on December 16, 1944, when Germany launched its attack. Keep in mind that this was after the Allies freed France, and they thought that Germany did not have the weapons and willpower to push back. Therefore, the attack came as somewhat of a surprise to the Allied powers. Hitler ordered his troops to attack through the Ardennes Forest in Belgium, a dense area of trees and marsh that made the movement of equipment difficult. The Allied forces had set up a line there from which they could attack should the enemy try to cross into freed territory. Given that the ambush was unexpected, the Germans were successful in pushing the Allied frontline back into the center. This created an uneven line that would look like a bugle when looking at a map. Again, Blitzkrieg was implemented, whereby Germany sent 200,000 troops and 1,000 tanks to cross the front *(Battle of Bulge,* n.d.). Similarly, the temperature was low, and the Americans also had to fight treacherous weather conditions. When the Germans made efficient advances, many American soldiers were killed, and some thought that the Germans might actually realize their battle objectives.

German machine gunner marching through the Ardennes in Battle of the Bulge,
1944

They used sneaky ways to ambush the enemy. For example, some English-speaking Germans were disguised as American soldiers and relayed false information to troops that confused and hindered their efforts. Nonetheless, American troops were determined to win and were not going to let the Germans push them out. They implemented guerrilla warfare, a war tactic characterized by small groups of people who attack from unusual locations. This proved to be effective, and many Germans fell prey to this method. German soldiers gave Americans the opportunity to surrender, but they never took it. Instead, they continued fighting back and kept the Germans from advancing further. It was only a small group of Americans who dug a trench and held the big German army from going deeper into the interior. They bravely kept them out while waiting for more reinforcements to assist them in battle. Once reinforcements arrived, the Allied powers quickly got control of the situation and fought until the Germans surrendered on January 25, 1945. The bravery of American troops was so impressive that Winston Churchill once remarked, "This is undoubtedly the greatest American battle of the war and will, I believe, be regarded as an ever-famous American victory" (*Battle of the Bulge*, 2020). Sadly, their bravery came at a price. Some 19,000 American soldiers lost their lives during the conflict. Yet, they will always be remembered as heroically fending off the Nazis and changing the trajectory of the war.

The Battle of Berlin

The Battle of Berlin was the beginning of the end. It was the last major battle of World War Two and ended with Germany's total surrender, which ultimately concluded the six years of conflict. In essence, it was the last stand by the Germans as the Allied powers entered the capital city, Berlin. The battle officially began on April 16, 1945, when the city was surrounded by the Soviet army. The Soviets had made many advances as the war neared its end and frequently attacked German towns on their way to Berlin. Many German civilians were killed, and the government even spread information on how to commit suicide if the Russians approached one's land. Hitler grew increasingly paranoid and hid in his underground bunker in Berlin while the Soviet bombs were dropped from above. Nevertheless, Nazi officials expected the German people to stay loyal to their nation and die in the name of victory. In his last speech, the Nazi Propaganda Minister, Joseph Goebbels, stated, "Germany is still the land of loyalty; it will celebrate its greatest triumphs in the midst of danger; never will history record that in these days a people deserted its führer [leader]!" (Letts, 2016, p. 182). It was the first time many Germans saw the reality of war as the Russians entered the city with 2,500,000 soldiers and 6,250 tanks (*Battle of Berlin*, 2019).

Russian soldier raising Soviet flag over the Nazi Reichstag chancellery during the Battle of Berlin, 1945

Many German soldiers were injured, had no weapons, and were simply tired. The force was depleted, but they were expected to stand up and face the enemy head-on. From his bunker, Hitler ordered everyone in the city to join the fight: elderly people, women, and children. In fact, the last photograph of Hitler shows him awarding a teenage boy a medal for bravery. The Germans had no strategy, and many opted to fight by hand or run away. German authorities severely punished those civilians who attempted to escape by executing them and hanging them in the streets of the capital. The closer the Russians got, the more dire the situation became. Many German civilians killed themselves after years of indoctrination concerning supposed Russian brutality. After the war ended, the Allied powers were shocked to find large numbers of government officials and ordinary citizens who lay dead at their own hands. By April 30, Hitler knew there was no hope and committed suicide in his bunker with his wife, Eva Braun. However, he did not accept defeat and passed his power on to Karl Dönitz. Dönitz knew that if Germany did not surrender, the whole nation would soon be annihilated. On May 7, the German leaders who were still alive signed documents of unconditional surrender, and the war finally came to a close. During the battle, about 92,000 German soldiers, 81,000 Russians, and 22,000 German civilians lost their lives (*Battle of Berlin*, 2019).

A devastated Berlin street just off the Unter den Linden after Battle of Berlin, 1945

The Story of Sergei Aleshkov

A witness to one of these battles was a child named Sergei Aleshkov. At a young age, he witnessed the Battle of Stalingrad and even helped his comrades during the fighting. Sergei was born in the Soviet village of Gryn in either 1934 or 1936. The village was very poor, and most families survived through subsistence farming. That being said, everyone was on high alert when war broke out. Gryn became a base for partisans, whereby the inhabitants were known to harbor fighters and provided them with food. Once the Germans invaded in the summer of 1942, the villagers did not know what hit them. The small Sergei saw Russian fighters and his beloved family members being murdered mercilessly. His mother was shot, and his 10-year-old brother was hanged, leaving him utterly alone. The 6- or 8-year-old climbed through the window and ran into the forest. He was lucky that he survived, but now he was to wander in the forest with no food or warmth. No one really knows how long Sergei was in the forest, only that he was found by Soviet troops who took the young boy to their army base. Troops described him as being very shy and crying profusely about his mother. Upon realizing that he was an orphan, the infantry adopted him and ensured that he got a perfectly-sized Soviet uniform. Sergei made a significant impression on Major Mikhail Vorobyov, who had no family of his own. In time, Vorobyov became Sergei's adoptive father and married a medical officer called Nina Bedova. Sergei had a new family with two loving parents, albeit in a very strange scenario.

During the rest of the war, Sergei served as an assistant to his adoptive father. He would go to the base headquarters every morning and get a rundown of his daily assignments. Due to his age, he was usually tasked with carrying messages between officers or delivering newspapers. In times of active battle, he carried grenades and cartridges. However, he quickly achieved success as a spotter after noticing suspicious individuals hidden in a haystack who turned out to be Germans. On one occasion, Sergei even saved his adoptive father's life when he was stuck under rubble after a German attack. Sergei took an active role in the Battle of Stalingrad, where he fell under mortar fire. He was wounded when shrapnel hit his leg but returned to the frontlines immediately after receiving treatment. Not only that, but he also almost drowned in the Donets River, almost stepped on a landmine, and was almost shot by German pilots after wearing a lieutenant's uniform in jest. Luckily, he made it out of the war physically unharmed. The family of three subsequently moved to Chelyabinsk, where Sergei excelled in school. He studied law and worked in the prosecutor's office. He would go on to marry and raise two children. He died of a heart attack in 1990. Sergei is the perfect example of the power a child or a teenager holds. If Sergei could get through all of these calamities, you are strong enough to survive anything!

Key Takeaways

- There were thousands of battles during World War Two. However, some particularly stand out due to their high death toll and the impact they had in changing the course of the war.

- The Battle of Dunkirk mostly consisted of the evacuation of British troops from France and resulted in a German victory.

- The Battle of France led to Germany taking over the nation of France and boosted German morale for continued European expansion.

- The Battle of Midway was a conflict in the Pacific Ocean between the Americans and the Japanese, where the former destroyed all their aircraft carriers and resulted in dampening Japanese influence in the region.

- The Battle of Stalingrad started when Germany tried to annex Russia, but the Russians fought back and trapped them within the city of Stalingrad. German troops were starved and consequently surrendered.

- The Battle of Bulge was Germany's last effort to push the Allied forces out of Europe. They attacked through the Ardennes Forest, but American soldiers bravely fended them off and assured Allied victory.

- The Battle of Berlin was the final battle of World War Two as the Soviet Union entered the capital of Germany. Everyone in the city fought back, but the Soviets were stronger. It led to Hitler's suicide and the end of the war.

CHAPTER 4:

Leaders and Heroes

"FORMER AMERICAN PRESIDENT JOHN F. KENNEDY SAID, "One person can make a difference, and everyone should try" (Ludwig, 2018, p. 142). This quote is especially true in times of war. Every nation that fought in World War Two was led by a president, prime minister, or king. Even so, the many branches that made up their respective militaries were led by men at the helm. Their orders navigated the path the war took, and they held the lives of countless soldiers and civilians in their hands. Some of these leaders were heroic, whereas others are remembered as controversial stains on world history. It is important to know who these men were as it gives you an idea of the reasoning behind the efforts they took. For instance, it is easy to get wrapped up in the battle stories and conflict situations of a participating country like Japan. But did you know that Japan was ruled by Emperor Hirohito, who had to sign off on the planned attack on Pearl Harbor? By looking at these men, you will better understand the circumstances that continued the war effort. Just as it is important to know who the leaders were, so is it to focus on the many heroes that fought for positive change during World War Two. There were individuals who single-handedly changed the tide of war, those who saved many soldiers from certain death, and those who risked their own lives to save Jews during the Holocaust. You might also be surprised to find that there were several German heroes who did their part in ending the evil Nazi regime from within. You should never fall into the mindset of thinking people from one nationality or ethnicity are all the same when learning about topics like World War Two. The entire war was made up of individuals who worked together so that they could reach their goals, whether that be heinous or admirable. So, let's take a look at some of these individuals. We will start with the leaders first.

Axis and Allied Leaders

The most famous leader of the Axis powers was, of course, Adolf Hitler. We discussed him in Chapter One. So, let's focus on the two respective leaders of Italy and Japan and observe how their personalities contributed to their conduct during the war.

Benito Mussolini was the dictator of Italy during World War Two. As a child, Mussolini was described as a bully and was heavily influenced by his father's political views. The boy grew up supporting the ideology of fascism, an idea that a country should be ultranationalist and be ruled by an autocratic leader. In 1919, he started the Fascism Party, which grew in support. Devoted male members were known as "Black Shirts" and terrorized those who did not follow Mussolini's ideas. In 1922, the Black Shirts marched into the capital city of Rome and took control by force. In three years, Mussolini had full power and became a vicious dictator. Just like Hitler's wish for Germany, Mussolini wanted Italy to rule Europe and build up its military strength so that it could be more powerful on the world stage. Hitler and Mussolini were friends because they admired each other's toughness and ruthlessness. When Italy joined the Axis powers in 1940, they were not ready for war, but Mussolini was convinced that they would be victorious. He boldly proclaimed, "War is to man what maternity is to woman. From a philosophical and doctrinal viewpoint, I do not believe in perpetual peace" (Bali, 2013, p. 173). Simply put, he was hungry for battle and ordered his troops to realize the bigger goal of Italian expansion. Yet, Italian citizens were dismayed at the many losses and wanted out of the conflict. In 1943, Italian leaders managed to jail Mussolini, that is, until Hitler freed him and put him in charge of territory under German control! On April 28, 1945, Mussolini saw that the war was coming to an end. He tried to escape by disguising himself but was soon caught by Italian soldiers. They executed him and hung his body upside down over a gas station in Milan. A violent end to a violent man.

Benito Mussolini, "Il Duce", 1938

During World War Two, Japan was ruled by Emperor Hirohito. The Japanese believed that he was a divine being who had the right to rule as he saw fit. Japanese culture places heavy emphasis on loyalty, and most citizens thought that Emperor Hirohito had their best intentions at heart. When he was born in 1901, his grandfather was emperor, and he sent the young Hirohito to Europe to learn about the West. Surprisingly, during the trip, he did not visit Germany, which he was to align with during the war! After both his grandfather and father died, he became emperor in 1926. While in this position, he thought his role should be to listen to his advisors, most of whom were military leaders who wanted to expand Japanese influence. Not following their orders could lead to an assassination, and he reluctantly agreed to the invasion of China in 1937. Following the advice of his advisors, he joined the Axis powers in 1940 so that they could continue Japanese expansion in the Pacific. He personally signed off on the attack on Pearl Harbor and was proud when his nation annexed the Philippines. By 1942, Japan was increasingly defeated in battle, and Hirohito feared for the future of his country. Yet, he remained loyal to the Japanese war efforts and refused to surrender. At the start of 1945, the Japanese had lost all their territory that was gained during the war and were in a bad economic state. Nevertheless, Japan did not even surrender when the other Axis powers did. Hirohito only ceased conflict when the United States dropped two atomic bombs on the Japanese cities of Hiroshima and Nagasaki in August 1945. Of course, the Allied powers wanted to see him be prosecuted for his involvement, but American leaders thought his removal would lead to mayhem. Instead, they removed his powers, and he stayed on as a ceremonial emperor until his death from cancer in 1989. The Axis powers, therefore, had vastly different leaders who worked together to defeat the Allied powers.

Emperor Hirohito of Japan, 1926-1989

The Allied leaders are viewed more favorably as they were staunchly opposed to the Nazi ideology. The leaders of the "big three" will be the focus. Although Britain entered the war when their prime minister was Neville Chamberlain, Winston Churchill replaced him in 1940 and led the nation for the majority of the conflict. Today, there are many monuments to Prime Minister Churchill, who is believed to have saved Britain in its darkest hour. Churchill was a military man who escaped a prison camp during the Second Boer War in 1899. His survival story caught the attention of many Brits who wanted a fighter in power.

Chamberlain seemed to cozy up to Hitler throughout the 1930s in a supposed attempt to appease him diplomatically. Churchill was the right man to fight and succeeded Chamberlain a year after the war began. When he became prime minister, he was fully aware that his primary role was to ensure British victory. In his first speech, he said, "I have nothing to offer but blood, toil, tears, and sweat" (Morson, 2011, p. 143). He expected his countrymen to follow suit and fight for their country, no matter the circumstances. Churchill despised Hitler and strategized from his office at 10 Downing Street to make sure that Germany never set foot on British soil. During the Battle of Britain, he boosted morale so that the Royal Air Force could counter German air attacks. Britain won. Similarly, during the bombing campaign known as the "Blitz," he comforted his citizens and made sure that everyone had an air raid shelter they could go to. This period of British history was difficult, but Churchill never lost hope and encouraged citizens to follow his example. He was also instrumental in negotiating the Allied alliance and made several hostile countries come to the table so that they could stand together against Hitler. His tireless efforts ultimately paid off and are a big reason why the Allies won. After the war, he remained active in politics and even became the prime minister again in 1951. He passed away on January 24, 1965.

Winston Churchill, UK Prime Minister, 1943

President Franklin D. Roosevelt led the United States from 1933 to 1945, the entire length of Hitler's reign in Germany. Roosevelt was a highly educated man and quickly impressed the American public when he entered politics in 1910. In 1921 he was struck with polio and could only walk short distances thereafter. He was in a wheelchair, but this was definitely not a sign of weakness! He first served as the successful governor of New York and then won the presidential election in 1932. This was during the Great Depression, and Roosevelt had the enormous responsibility of managing the economy. His responsive policies were effective and helped the nation in immeasurable ways. Many government programs Americans enjoy today—such as social security—are due to Roosevelt's effort in combating the Great Depression. He was so invested in these national matters that he did not want to enter World War Two. Yet, he offered financial support and weapons to Britain. When the Japanese attacked Pearl Harbor, he knew it was time to act. In a congressional speech, he characterized the assault as "A date that will live in infamy" (Benford, 2001, p. 66). Once involved, he supervised every aspect of America's war effort. He mobilized the economy to fund their military actions and enacted the Europe First strategy that promoted a close relationship with Britain. Roosevelt also used American innovation to stimulate the production of nuclear weapons in the form of atomic bombs that were eventually dropped on Japan. Like Churchill, Roosevelt knew how important the relationship between the Allies was and hosted several summits and promoted constructive dialogue to ensure a unified approach. Additionally, he was instrumental in sowing the seeds for the formation of the United Nations in the aftermath of war. Sadly, his administration was criticized for their policy of interning Japanese–Americans, whom they feared posed a risk to national security. Nonetheless, he is remembered as an important figure that turned the tide on Hitler. He died of a stroke a month before the war ended, but luckily his efforts in the years prior cemented the victory America saw in April 1945.

Franklin D Roosevelt, President of the USA, 1933

Perhaps the most controversial Allied leader was Josef Stalin of the Soviet Union. When Stalin was young, it was his dream to be a priest, but he was expelled from seminary because he was thought to be too "radical." He loved communist writings, such as those by Karl Marx, and wanted a new political ideology to take hold in Russia. He established a friendship with Vladimir Lenin, who led the Russian Revolution in 1917 that ousted the monarchy. When Lenin was in power, Stalin was awarded a high-ranking position, and when the former died, Stalin followed him as the sole leader of the Soviet Union. He is believed to have been a dictator because he actively murdered other political leaders who disagreed with him or threatened his grasp on power. His industrial and agricultural policies were also controversial because they led to more than 6 million Russian deaths *(Biography: Joseph Stalin*, 2018). He thought that the industrialization of his nation was more important than the civilian deaths it led to. Although this was tragic, the rapid development of the Soviet Union put them in a position to protect the country from Germany. Stalin had first aligned himself with Hitler so that he could get a section of Poland. But, when Hitler went against his word and attacked the Soviet Union, Stalin was furious. Josef had set up a cult of personality, and Soviet citizens were required to worship him. What would it look like if Germany annexed a part of the country that he was divinely leading? His cult of personality is one reason why the Soviets fought so harshly. They wanted to protect their nation, in addition to their hero Stalin. Stalin was personally responsible for every action his nation undertook and planned military strategies with his government officials. He regularly made speeches that emboldened citizens to keep up the fight and was delighted when his soldiers protected their borders so efficiently. Stalin was not pleased with having to align himself with Western countries that supported political ideologies he found abhorrent, but it was necessary if he was to protect the Soviet Union. After the war, his relationship with his former allies soured drastically. Stalin used the opportunity of European uncertainty to take power in several Eastern European nations and the eastern half of Germany. His competition and hatred for America also led to the Cold War that lasted long after his death. Although he died in 1953, communism thrived in the Soviet Union and Eastern European countries until 1989.

Joseph Stalin, Leader of the Soviet Union, 1942

As you have seen, the personalities that made up the Allied Powers were unique. The only Allied unifier was that all these leaders wanted to ensure that the Nazis did not win.

Allied Heroes

The landscape of World War Two was scattered with heroes. Military officials, troops, and civilians were shocked at the atrocities caused by the Nazis and who did their best to turn the tide of war. As we will see, there were even some German heroes who wanted to bring about the downfall of Hitler and his hateful regime. If we can learn anything from them, it is that any individual can make a difference and fight for positive change. That being said, being in a position of power allows for a greater capacity to enact change, which is why we will be looking at two military heroes first. The first is General George Patton from the United States. He was one of the most heroic generals and was jokingly referred to as "old blood and guts!" As a child, he loved listening to stories about his ancestors who fought in the American Civil War and yearned to be just like them when he grew up. He immediately joined the army when he left school and made a name for himself when he participated in the killing of a Mexican revolutionary. Particularly because he convinced his fellow troops to tie three corpses from the ambush onto their automobiles! During World War One, he became an expert in tank warfare, and when America joined World War Two, he was shipped to command troops in Europe. By all accounts, he was ready for battle and even got an airplane license so that he could monitor his tanks from above. He once said, "Wars may be fought with weapons, but they are won by men. It is the spirit of men who follow and of the man who leads that gains victory" (Matthews, 2020, p. 197). He believed strongly that troops under his command should be obedient and listen attentively to his instructions. In fact, he was suspended for a while because he was considered too harsh on his subordinates. Yet, he led the invasion of Italy and took 100,000 enemy soldiers captive (*Biography: George Patton*, 2019). Nazi leaders are said to have feared the mention of Patton's name as he never lost a battle under his command. One of his most impressive accomplishments was during the Battle of Bulge. He rescued Allied troops in Belgium and led his troops to reinforce Allied lines with speed. After the Germans were sufficiently pushed back, he ordered his troops to follow him into the interior of Germany. His successful leadership of his 300,000 soldiers is evidenced by the fact that they captured an estimated 1.5 million German troops as they walked deeper into the country. Sadly, months after the war ended, Patton was killed in a car crash. Today, he is remembered as an American hero that made an Allied victory more likely.

General George Patton, 1945

Another heroic military leader was Georgy Zhukov from the Soviet Union. When he was born to a poor, peasant Russian family, they certainly did not expect him to become as successful as he became.

During World War One, he made a name for himself as one of the most effective soldiers, and he was actively involved in the Russian Revolution of 1917. He was a staunch communist who wanted to protect this political ideology from Nazi intrusion. When World War Two started, he was appointed as the chief of staff of the Red Army. He strategized the defense of Leningrad and Moscow in 1941. He tasked his troops to work with civilians and fight back against the Nazis as a unified force. It was Zhukov who ensured a Soviet victory at the Battle of Kursk and prevented German advances on Soviet territory. He operated from the standpoint that sometimes less is more. For instance, Zhukov knew that the cold temperature in the Soviet Union was something German troops were not used to and opted to trap Germans so that his troops did not have to meet unnecessary deaths. The strategy employed during the Battle of Stalingrad was Zhukov's idea and ultimately led to a Soviet defeat. Sometimes, he was in conflict with Stalin as Zhukov was a man of his own mind who shared his opposing views openly. However, Stalin knew how effective Zhukov was and consistently asked him for help when a situation needed military intervention. Zhukov was also the man that led the Soviets through modern-day Belarus into Germany for the final assault on Berlin. He commanded his troops to continue the fighting and identified the areas where they would be most effective. You can imagine the triumphant feeling Zhukov had when Germany surrendered! When the war ended, Stalin was understandably worried about the high regard in which citizens Russians held Zhukov. Feeling threatened, Stalin appointed Zhukov to regional commands far from the Soviet capital, Moscow. Zhukov died on June 18, 1974, and is considered one of the Russian greats by historians. Zhukov and Patton were heroic men who made their marks in history. In saying that, there are many more military heroes, such as Britain's Bernard Montgomery, that you can read about! Furthermore, there was also a wide array of heroes whom you do not regularly read about in history books.

Georgy Zhukov, 1944

One of these lesser-known heroes was an Irish man named Richard Hayes. Before the war started, Richard Hayes lived a quiet family life and worked as a librarian. He was also a highly-acclaimed mathematician but enjoyed his life out of the limelight. In the early days of the conflict, Hayes did not expect that his life would be upended as his native Ireland had a policy of remaining neutral and did not support either side in the conflict. That all changed when the intelligence services found out that Hayes was a man with a talent for codebreaking. During the war, the Allied and Axis powers used codes to communicate with each other, and enemies struggled to identify what they were telling each other. Ireland supported the Allied efforts from afar so that the Nazis would not arrive on their shores. Intelligence forces were very worried about Nazi spies who went to Ireland so that they could relay information to Germany on strategic spots in the country. Hayes first impressed the intelligence forces when he interrogated and broke the code of the German spy Wilhelm Preetz in 1941. Perhaps Hayes's biggest achievements were through his interrogations of Günther Schütz and Hermann Goertz. Code breakers could not decipher their secret messages, but Hayes used the information he received when he questioned them and used it to successfully analyze their systems of microdots and uncover the sensitive information they held. Hayes was definitely not a military man, but his attention to detail and ability to break numerous German codes assisted the British military in knowing what the Germans were planning so they could prepare for responses. Hayes was a true hero who should be awarded gratitude for helping to protect the Allies from the Nazis.

In a time when women were not considered appropriate for military service, one Soviet woman stood out and became a hero in her own right. Her name was Lyudmila Pavlichenko. She became known as "Lady Death" due to her remarkable talent in shooting. In 1941, she was only 24 and studying at university. But when she heard about Hitler's invasion of her country, she quickly left her studies and enlisted in the army. Soviet officials wanted to make her a nurse, but she insisted on joining the troops. Her role was as a sniper, whereby she would hide and shoot the enemy when they approached. Her fellow male troops underestimated her when she arrived, but she ended up being more successful than them! During the German attack on a

Soviet town called Sevastopol, she shot more enemy soldiers than any other sniper surrounding her. In May 1942, she had already recorded 257 kills which afforded her the title of lieutenant. The more enemy troops she killed, the more she was sent to increasingly dangerous battles. During these battles, she was wounded at least four times, yet she always returned to fight for her country. The Germans were aware of her and tried to bribe her into joining their forces. A message to her read, "Lyudmila Pavlichenko, come over to us; we will give you plenty of chocolate and make you a German officer!" (Gentry, 2021). She laughed them off and was delighted that the Germans feared her. Lyudmila survived the war and lived on as a hero until she died in 1974.

An unusual hero was the American Virginia Hall. As a young girl, she thrived on adventure and did not want to follow in the footsteps of other girls in her wealthy community. She opted to study in France and fell in love with the country. She thought that her adventurous personality would best be fostered if she became a diplomat. While serving as a U.S. diplomat, she had a hunting accident that resulted in the amputation of her foot. However, this did not stop her. When Germany invaded France, she offered to drive an ambulance but went to Britain when France sadly fell. There, she met up with the British intelligence who sent her to France under the pretense of being a reporter. Once there, she organized French resistance forces and infiltrated areas where German troops discussed important matters. No one thought that a thin, handicapped woman was a threat to their war goals! Throughout her time in France, she constantly changed her appearance so that the dreaded Gestapo—the Nazi police force— would not catch and execute her. In time, the Gestapo caught wind of the woman who was relaying secret information to the Allies. They set up posters with her face on them that stated, "The enemy's most dangerous spy—we must find and destroy her!" (Myre, 2019). They were nearing in on her when she escaped to Spain and then Britain. Yet, her heart was in France, and she went back as the war was nearing its end. Back in France, Virginia's network of resistance consisted of an estimated 1,500 people who reclaimed areas and sabotaged German efforts even before Allied troops entered the country. After the war, she returned to the United States, where she lived until her death in 1982. Her heroic efforts will always be remembered with fondness by the French. Although she was not a native-born citizen, she was instrumental in freeing France from tyranny. Do you see? All of us can make a difference!

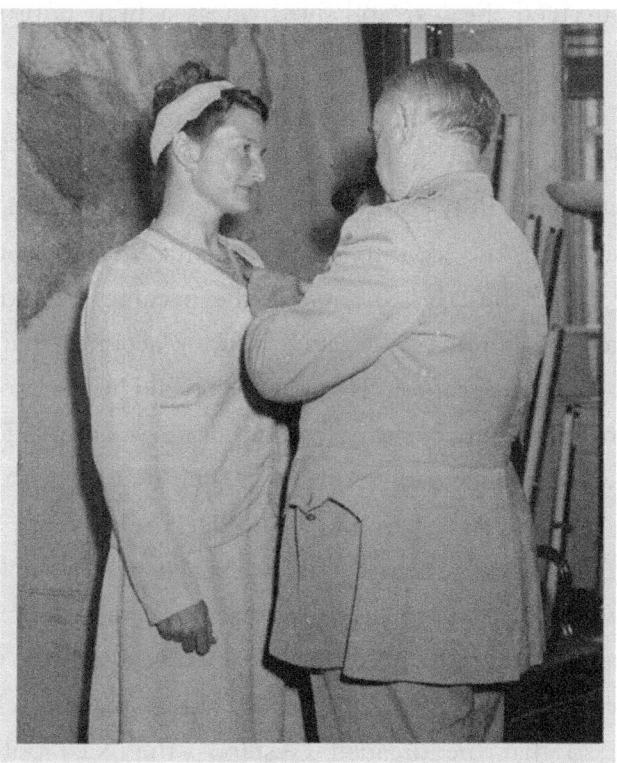

Virginia Hall of Special Operations Branch receiving the Distinguished Service Cross from General Donovan, 1945

The Story of Hans and Sophie Scholl

When thinking about World War Two, it is very easy to fall into groupthink. Namely, Germany—and its citizens—was the "big bad wolf," and every German was an enthusiastic fan of Hitler and his beliefs. This is unfortunate because many Germans did not agree with the course their nation took, and some civilians even tried to bring down the regime. Two of these people were the German siblings Hans and Sophie Scholl. Hans and Sophie were once Nazi youth leaders but became disillusioned with the regime after seeing the horrific effects of Hitler's policies. They helped form a German resistance group known as the "White Rose," who wanted to end the war and Hitler's grip on power. During this period, the Nazis did not allow any dissent, and they risked their lives in standing up to the country's leaders. Hans and Sophie were both university students aged 24 and 21, respectively, but they were more interested in changing German opinions about Hitler than their coursework. They organized many underground meetings where German resistance members would come together and work on plans to get their message across. One way in which this was done was through publishing their writings in secret. Hans and Sophie, together with other individuals like Christoph Probst, wrote anti-Nazi pamphlets and distributed them in people's mailboxes at night. It was very dangerous as the Gestapo was routinely on the lookout for dissenting opinions. They were successful at first, but all of it erupted on February 18, 1943.

On that day, Hans and Sophie entered the University of Munich with 1,700 anti-Nazi pamphlets hidden in a suitcase. They originally planned to place them outside each classroom, but when they realized that they had 100 left, they went to the top of the atrium's gallery and threw them into the large foyer. Sadly, a janitor noticed the pair, and the Gestapo arrested them as they stood frozen. Hans, Sophie, and

Christoph—who was arrested at the White Rose Office of Operation—were sent to court in what was ultimately a mock trial. Everyone knew that speaking out against Hitler always led to execution. During her interrogation, Sophie remained calm and confessed to her actions, refusing to say that she had done anything wrong. When the fanatical Nazi judge, Roland Freisler, asked her whether she thought she committed a crime, she said, "I am, now as before, of the opinion that I did the best that I could do for my nation; I, therefore, do not regret my conduct and will bear the consequences that result from my conduct" (Spitzer, 2020). Hans and Sophie suffered horrific verbal abuse from Freisler, who accused them of being traitors and said that he would not spare them from harsh judgment. A mere four days after their arrest, Hans, Sophie, and Christoph were executed by guillotine. They are remembered through several memorial plaques at the university, where they acted so heroically in 1943. Although they did not see the end of the war, they proved that many Germans were good people and despised the heinous actions undertaken by Nazi leaders. They teach us that we should always stand up for what is right, no matter the circumstances that threaten to silence us.

Brother and sister Hans and Sophie Scholl, 1943

Key Takeaways

- The Axis leaders were Adolf Hitler of Germany, Benito Mussolini of Italy, and Emperor Hirohito of Japan.

- The Allied leaders were Winston Churchill of Great Britain, Franklin D. Roosevelt of the United States, and Josef Stalin of the Soviet Union.

- Two heroic Allied military heroes were the American General George Patton and the Soviet Commander Georgy Zhukov. The former was responsible for the speed of his attacks, particularly in the Battle of Bulge, and the latter oversaw all the major Soviet battles effectively.

- Not all heroes adorned a military uniform. The Irish librarian, Richard Hayes, was a successful code breaker who kept Britain safe; the Soviet Lyudmila Pavlichenko was a successful sniper who killed many enemy fighters, and the American Virginia Hall was instrumental in organizing the French resistance.

CHAPTER 5:

The Tragedy That Was the Holocaust

AN AUSCHWITZ CONCENTRATION CAMP SURVIVOR, Sara Zuchowski, remembered, "They brought us into Auschwitz. I could see chimneys burning, smell the smoke. I did not think about it. They gave us tattoos: 33076. I did not have a name anymore; just a number" (Zuchowski, 2020). Unbeknownst to Sara at the time, the smoke she smelled was the remains of murdered Jewish individuals who were systematically gassed in death chambers. The elimination of all Jews was one of the primary goals of Adolf Hitler. An estimated six million Jews were killed in what is now known as the Holocaust. It was the largest mass extermination campaign ever seen in the history of the world, and generations of people were wiped from the face of the earth. This begs the question: Why did Hitler hate Jews? And how could anyone follow his orders to kill men, women, and children on such a scale? The answers to these questions are complex but can generally be attributed to four broad reasons. Firstly, religious conflict. Followers of Judaism have been discriminated against for centuries. Throughout history, they have been expelled, killed, and ethnically profiled due to the belief that they were responsible for the crucifixion of the Christian messiah, Jesus. Secondly, supposed economic power. Hitler and many Nazi followers were angry that a wide swath of German banks and institutions were owned and managed by Jews. This belief is also related to the racist notion that Jews have a desire for wealth. Thirdly, conspiracy theories. Because Jews were prominent in business circles and did not seem to suffer as much as other Germans during the Great Depression, the Nazis felt that the entire Jewry wanted to control Germany and eventually the world. Fourthly, biological differences. Hitler and other Nazis thought that ethnic Jews were a completely separate race. Hitler held the view that some races were better than others, and Jews were considered at the lowest level of this hierarchy. Nazism promoted the idea that if Germany was to thrive, citizens with a German bloodline—called Aryans—should be protected from "Jewish infestation." Hitler wrote, "For a racially pure people which is conscious of its blood can never be enslaved by the Jew" (Koeningsberg, 2007, p. 28). He thought that Jews had inferior blood that should not mix with "pure" Germans if they were to be the strongest group of people on the earth.

Hitler clearly outlined his beliefs in his book, *Mein Kampf*, which he urged everyone to read. He used mass propaganda to spread these beliefs and used inaccurate and offensive portrayals of Jews to garner support for his racist objectives. Additionally, as many European Jews were successful, he hoped that the state could take control of their assets and use it to help the Aryan population prosper economically. That being said, Hitler espoused hatred for more than just Jews. He wanted to rid the world of any individual who was not the "perfect" Aryan. That is why he enacted hostile policies toward homosexuals, black people, and those with physical disabilities, to name only three. It is important to note that all these beliefs are false and intensely hurtful. No person is born superior to another, and the Holocaust is the perfect example of what can happen when this wicked attitude takes hold in mainstream society. The full-blown extermination of Jews was not the first step the Nazis undertook when they came to power. Rather, Hitler slowly built up the hostility through policies that became more atrocious the longer he stayed in power. You're about to learn about the entire process that led up to the mass extermination of millions of innocent human beings.

Early Anti-Semitic Policies and Ghettos

As soon as the Nazis came to power, they immediately started enacting anti-Semitic policies. *Anti-Semitism* is a term that describes prejudice against Jewish individuals. In this context, early policies refer to those made before the outbreak of World War Two. They are divided into three distinct periods, with each being more aggressive than the former. The first phase lasted from 1933 to 1934. During this time, a civil service law was enacted that prohibited any Jewish person from holding a government job. Jews were no longer allowed to teach in public schools or universities, be state lawyers or work in government hospitals. Not only that, but the government also urged German citizens to boycott Jewish-owned shops or from doing any sort of business with them. A cultural shift also took place, whereby the curriculum in schools was modified to include lessons on race that promoted discrimination. Moreover, Germans were encouraged to hold bonfire parties where they would burn books written by influential Jewish writers, and Jews were further prohibited from holding a job in any cultural setting, such as in the radio or the theater. The second period lasted from 1935 to 1936 and saw the enactment of the Nuremberg Laws. These laws identified who was to be classified as a Jew. It did not matter whether a person followed Judaism; all that mattered was whether they had "Jewish blood." The Nazis agreed that anyone with at least one Jewish grandparent should be classified as such and consequently be discriminated against. The most shocking element of these new laws was that Jews were no longer considered citizens of Germany. They were enemies and had no right to national protection that a citizen is afforded. Similarly, it was forbidden for Jews to have relations with non-Jews, and the societal divide grew larger and larger.

Nazi boycott of Jewish stores, probably Berlin, Germany, 1933

The third period lasted from 1937 to 1939. This characterized the full removal of Jews from society. In 1937, the state actively confiscated many Jewish-owned businesses and property and encouraged business owners to dismiss Jews from working for them. Additionally, Nazis required all Jews to have a stamp on their identification papers and passports that classified their "race." They were forbidden from attending any cultural gathering, such as concerts, were no longer entitled to have driver's licenses or phones, and even had restrictions on the amount of money they could have in their bank accounts! The Night of the Broken Glass was a cultural turning point when it became acceptable for the average citizen to physically attack any Jewish person. On November 9, 1938, Nazi officials and citizens participated in burning down 1,400 synagogues and destroying 7,000 stores that were still owned by Jews (Anti-Semitism Globally, 2005). By the end of that year, all Jewish stores were ordered to close down, and Jewish children were no longer allowed to go to school. Thousands of Jews emigrated, but most were unable to leave due to a lack of funds or immigration quotas in other countries. Those that stayed were ordered to leave their homes and find supposed refuge in ghettos.

A burning synagogue, during Kristallnacht, Baden-Baden, 1938

The first ghetto was built by the Germans in Poland after the start of the war. When any country was annexed, it naturally fell under Nazi laws, and there was no difference between a German or any other European Jew. In fact, most ghettos were built in Eastern Europe, and German Jews were transported to those regularly. Ghettos were horrible places to live because they were overcrowded, there was not enough food, and there was a limited number of jobs. The Warsaw Ghetto in Poland had 400,000 Jews living in an area of 1.3 square miles (Ghettos, 2019)! In time, the Germans built more until a total of 1,143 European ghettos emerged, with more inhabitants arriving in each on a daily basis (Ghettos, 2019). All of the ghettos were surrounded by high walls that ensured the inhabitants did not mix with people outside. It was also during this time that Jews were required to wear a yellow star sewn into their clothes. This way, they were marked and would be spotted if they wandered outside of the ghetto walls. German authorities used inhabitants as slave labor to help in the war effort. It is difficult to imagine how they felt making weapons to help a country that was discriminating against them so profusely. Large ghettos were run by Jewish councils and police forces who followed the orders of German authorities. This resulted in many societal problems as the oppressors were now in their own communities. Unfortunately, the hard life in the ghetto was soon to be replaced by incarceration in concentration camps.

The Warsaw Ghetto, Poland, c.1940-43

Concentration Camps

In order to understand concentration camps, we must first look at their definition as used by the Nazis. During Nazi rule, a concentration camp was defined as "a camp in which people were detained or confined, usually under harsh conditions and without regard to legal norms of arrest or imprisonment" (*Nazi camps*, 2009.). In other words, they were facilities where all the enemies of Nazi Germany were held with no legal basis for being there. The first concentration camp was set up in 1933 and was called Dachau. The main prisoners to be taken there were individuals who posed a threat to Nazi ideals, like German communists. However, after the Night of the Broken Glass, thousands of people were sent to concentration camps simply for being Jewish. Over time, the number of concentration camps grew, and their incarceration rates increased rapidly. There were three main purposes for these camps. Firstly, to hold enemies of the state and keep them away from the general public. Secondly, to use the inmates as slave labor without running the risk of noncompliance. And thirdly, to kill small numbers of people away from the public eye. The camps used solely for the purpose of exterminating Jews only came to light in 1941 when the Nazis implemented the "Final Solution," a topic you will learn about later in the chapter. At first, killing largely took place among those who were too weak or ill to work in slave labor. Inmates were routinely shot or transported to "euthanasia" facilities, where they were murdered by poisonous gas. Concentration camps were further differentiated between forced labor and prisoner-of-war camps, although both operated in a similar manner.

Munitions produced by the inmates of Dachau Concentration Camp for the Nazi war effort, c. 1943

All types of concentration camps followed a regular chain of command, which were run by the feared SS—Schutzstaffel—who swore personal allegiance to Hitler. Men and women were separated, and female SS guards were tasked with maintaining order among female inmates. Concentration camps were run by the commandant, who managed the camp from his headquarters a distance from the grounds. An example of one of these was Amon Goeth, who commanded the Plaszow concentration camp in Poland and was said to shoot inmates from his lavish residence. The commandant's staff spent a great deal of time at the headquarters, where they ate, slept, and organized the functioning of the camp. Below the commandant was the security police officer who ran the protection detention office. This officer received orders from the commandant and the central security office in Berlin. He and his subordinates were responsible for keeping records of the inmates, like how many arrived, how many were killed, and what items were retrieved from them. Below him was the commander of the protective detention camp. He ran the day-to-day responsibilities and took orders from the commandant. Administration and supply authorities followed him and handled things such as food supply and maintenance. Then came the SS physician and other doctors. In concentration camps, the doctors chose who was fit to work and performed heinous human experiments on inmates in the name of "war research." In discussing the chain of command, it might sound like a well-run organization. Yet, you should not forget that this structure led to death and destruction. Inmates were forced to sleep in lice-infested cabins, had insufficient food, worked all day long, and were constantly under threat of being killed. The SS guards assigned no value to their lives and killed inmates routinely. One SS guard, Irma Grese, who was the warden of the Bergen–Belsen female concentration camp, is believed to have tortured inmates with a plaited whip. Many inmates died of malnutrition and horrific abuse. Nevertheless, the brutality of these facilities was to become even more horrendous once they were converted to death camps around 1941.

Jewish women and children arrive at Auschwitz-Birkenau camp (1942)

The Extermination of Other "Undesirables"

As was previously mentioned, Hitler and the Nazis discriminated against many types of people. A variety of other "undesirable" individuals were sent to concentration camps, euthanized, and killed in extermination camps. When thinking about the Holocaust, it is only natural to think about Jews. Yet, this is a limited view, as many others fell prey to the Nazis. Every life has dignity, and we should shine a light on those who are often overlooked when discussing mass genocide. Three classes of people—separate from Jews—faced Nazi discrimination and murder. They consisted of political and religious outsiders, "asocial" individuals, and those with physical or mental disabilities. Let's look at each sequentially.

Political outsiders were all those who were viewed as a threat to Nazism. They included Europeans who followed the ideologies of communism, socialism, and democracy, among others. For example, the German communist leader, Ernst Thaelmann, had run the German Communist Party since 1925 and refused to denounce this ideology. He was subsequently sent to a concentration camp, where he was murdered in 1944. Nazis also sent Jehovah's Witnesses to concentration camps because followers of this faith refused to give the Hitler salute in public. Their faith dictated that they were not allowed to worship any earthly "savior," and Hitler did not want this sentiment to grow among the public. Hence, they were viewed as political/religious enemies because they failed to swear allegiance to Hitler and the Nazis. All the inmates of concentration camps were forced to wear a uniform with a colored triangle on the badge to classify their reasoning for being incarcerated. Broad political enemies wore red stars, whereas Jehovah's Witnesses wore purple stars. The number of deaths among political prisoners is not known because they constituted a large and different group of people, but the death toll for

Jehovah's Witnesses is estimated to be about 1,500 (Jehovah's Witnesses, n.d.).

The classification of an "asocial" individual was similarly broad. The general rule of thumb was that those who could not conform to Aryan society were placed here. Jews and targeted racial groups were put into this group because Nazis believed they had "inferior blood." One of the largest groups targeted was Roma and Sinti—whom the Nazis called Gypsies. Hitler believed that they were racially inferior and more inclined to become criminals. Anyone with Slavic roots was thought of in this way, and the Nazis wanted to eradicate them so that a pure Aryan society could take form. In concentration camps, they were forced to wear black triangles, and about 500,000 were murdered during the genocide (Warnock, 2020). Homosexuals were also classified as "asocial." The reasoning behind their discrimination was the false belief that once all of them were eliminated, homosexuality would die out. The Nazis placed heavy emphasis on one's ability to procreate and therefore viewed gay people as bringing nothing to society. In concentration camps, they wore pink triangles and suffered horrendous abuse by SS guards who thought they lived an abhorrent lifestyle. A well-known gay hero was Willem Arondeus from Holland. When the war started, he lived with his partner, and the couple joined the Dutch resistance when the Germans invaded. Willem was instrumental in falsifying identity papers to help Jews escape and even burnt down the building where the papers were held when the Nazis approached! When the Nazis caught him, he was executed. Right before his death, he yelled, "Homosexuals are not cowards!" (*Mosaic of victims: in depth*, 2023). The last group, "asocials," were those individuals who suffered from societal problems, such as homelessness or drug abuse. It was common for the Gestapo to gather them in the streets and transport them to concentration camps. Once there, they wore black or brown triangles. It is unknown how many of these individuals died, but it is estimated to be in the thousands.

As with Jews, the discrimination and ultimate murder of people with physical or mental disabilities started immediately when Hitler came to power. He was convinced that disabled people threatened the goal of a strong Aryan population. In 1933, a law was passed that allowed disabled individuals to be sterilized so that they did not bring children into the world. Oftentimes, victims did not even know they were being sterilized, as the operation was frequently disguised as something else. There are also accounts of disabled people being murdered in ambulances or through starvation, and in 1939, it became an active policy. When the war started, the program of "euthanasia" was in full force. Disabled children were taken from their homes—as part of the dreaded T4 program—with Nazi officials promising the parents that they were being sent to care facilities. In fact, they were sent to facilities where they were murdered by lethal injection, starvation, and poisonous gas. Adults were included in the process, and mental hospitals were "emptied" of patients on a regular basis. Their families were told that they died of pneumonia or illness, but as time progressed, more Germans became aware of the practice. How is it possible that every disabled person died of pneumonia merely weeks after being taken away? Around the time that Jews were being murdered en masse, six extermination facilities were exclusively used for those with disabilities. A large number of adults were sent to these killing centers, where they were killed in gas chambers in groups. It is thought that an estimated 250,000 disabled people were killed by the Nazis (*Disabled people*, 2019). A truly horrific statistic.

The Final Solution

We have already discussed the use of concentration camps and that it was common for Jews to be killed on a sporadic basis. However, the industrialized implementation of the Jewish genocide only occurred after 1941. Throughout the years of Nazi rule, Hitler was constantly faced with the question of how he was going to rid Europe of its Jewish inhabitants. Several Nazi leaders suggested they be sent to Madagascar. Yet, this was not feasible. Hitler also knew that most Jews did not have the finances or availability to emigrate. Ghettos were increasingly overcrowded, and there were not enough concentration camps for the millions of Jews living on the continent. This was when he came up with the horrific idea of extermination in a systematic fashion. It was known as the "Final Solution to the Jewish Question."

While building the concentration camps, Nazi architects had already built facilities that could possibly be used for this purpose, and the outbreak of war intensified the speed at which Hitler wanted to realize his evil goal. Six extermination camps were built throughout 1941, and some existing concentration camps were fitted with killing facilities. In early 1942, Nazi leaders came together at the Wannsee Conference and planned the ways in which Hitler's wish was to be realized. It was decided that all Jewish ghettos were to be strategically evacuated and the inhabitants be sent by train toward their deaths. The Auschwitz extermination camp was the largest and accounted for the murder of more than 1.1 million Jews (Frost, 2020). When people arrived at the extermination camps, they did not know what to expect, and sadly, the vast majority did not know that they would die that day. A clear pattern emerged in how the process of extermination took place.

After Jews were gathered from ghettos, they were sent to a train station where they were told to write their names on their luggage. The train was a cattle wagon of sorts with no windows, bathroom facilities, or food. Every compartment was overcrowded, and many Jews did not even survive the journey to the camp. Those who did were told to exit the train upon arrival and line up for a medical inspection. Men in one line and women in another. When they reached the front, an SS doctor would choose whether they looked fit enough for labor or whether they should be killed immediately. If the former was chosen, the individual was sent to a delousing station where their heads were shaved, they were covered with disinfectant, given a tattoo with an identifiable number, and given a striped uniform to wear. Their living quarters were similar to earlier concentration camps, but their treatment was even more dire. They had to do backbreaking work, and their only sustenance was watery soup and a morsel of bread once a day. If a laborer seemed weak or ill, they were sent to the gas chamber or shot on the spot.

Jews from Subcarpathian Rus, then part of Hungary, await selection on the ramp at Auschwitz II-Birkenau, (1944)

In the second scenario, after arrival, Jews were pointed in the direction of the gas chambers. Rows of people destined to die were marched to a dressing facility where they were stripped of their clothes. SS guards told them that it was a routine shower, and that they should remember where they kept their belongings so as to minimize panic. However, once they entered the chamber, it was enclosed, and an SS guard poured the poisonous gas—Zyklon B—into the structure. It would take time to kill those within the chamber, and the SS guards knew that everyone was dead when they heard no more screaming. Jewish prisoners were then tasked to enter and remove the bodies, whereafter, they were sent to the crematorium and burned. In both scenarios, their luggage was sorted by prisoners and sent back to Germany, where the items were sold or used by citizens. When reading this methodically, it is almost unfathomable to think about the terror these individuals endured. Each of them was a unique individual with the inherent right to life. After the war, SS guards said that they were only following orders from Nazi leaders. But it is very difficult to imagine how one person could do this to their fellow human. The six million Jews that were killed will forever live in the hearts of the Jewish community and beyond. "Never again" is a sentiment we all should share!

The Story of Eva Schloss

One of the people who lived through the horrors of Auschwitz was 15-year-old Eva Schloss. In fact, she arrived in Auschwitz on her birthday! Her story began in 1929 when she was born to a middle-class Jewish family in Austria's capital city, Vienna. She had one brother called Heinz, whom she adored. When the Germans invaded Austria and took power, life became grim for Eva's family. She remembered that her brother was severely beaten at school and had to leave due to the abuse. Her father frantically looked for the opportunity to emigrate, and the family soon left for Holland, which they hoped would not be annexed as well. By February 1940, the family was living there, and her father made a small income. When thinking of Holland, Eva said, "The Dutch were very welcoming. I thought we were going to be okay" (Gruenbaum, 2017). For two months, life was normal. Eva made a few friends at her new school and spent hours playing with her brother, whom she described as very artistic. When Holland was invaded in May, everything changed, and the family again fell under the discriminatory policies they experienced in Austria. They stayed home, struggling to survive, until 1942, when Jewish deportations were in full force. Eva and her family were forced to find hiding spots with sympathetic families willing to face the threat of being labeled co-conspirators. They moved around six or seven times until they were caught. While in hiding, Heinz spent time painting and composing music, albeit a very somber existence. The family was separated, and one day when Eva and her mother were visiting her father and brother; the Gestapo arrived and arrested all of them.

The entire family was hoarded onto the dreaded train ride to Auschwitz. Eva had trouble thinking about this as the conditions were terrible and caused nightmares. When they arrived in Auschwitz, Eva and her mother were separated from the rest of the family. "Put on my coat and hat," Eva's mother told her when they were waiting in line for the medical inspection. Her mother knew that children and elderly people were sent elsewhere and did not want to be separated from her daughter. Eva believed that this saved her life because it made her look older than 15. Fortunately, no one in the family was sent to the gas chambers that day. Nevertheless, they were now to endure the horrible circumstances of the extermination camp. There were many occasions when Eva almost died. She suffered from typhus and was routinely abused by the SS guards. She claimed that her survival was due to two things. Firstly, the intervention of her cousin, Minni, who was a nurse in Auschwitz and even removed their names from an extermination list on one occasion! And secondly, hope. Eva once said, "I survived through hope. Hope keeps us going" (Gruenbaum, 2017). Eva and her mother worked in the sorting facility of the camp, where they were tasked with unpacking the luggage of Jews sent to the gas chambers. She remembered the many photographs they retrieved from the bags that they were forced to burn. Regrettably, Eva's father and brother died during their incarceration, but she and her mother survived and went back to Holland after liberation. The only memory she had of Heinz was the many personal paintings that he had hidden in the attic in Holland. Eva eventually made her way to Britain, where she became a citizen years later. Reading stories about teenage victims of the Holocaust rightfully stirs up emotions. It is difficult to think about the many generations of future families that were wiped out. All we can do is honor them and be comforted by the hope that such a thing will never happen in the future.

Key Takeaways

- The reasoning behind Nazi hatred toward Jews was mainly due to four elements: A long history of anti-Semitism based on the belief that Jews were responsible for the killing of Jesus, that Jews were more economically powerful, conspiracy theories that Jews wanted to take over the world, and that ethnic Jews were an entirely different race that was inferior to Aryan Germans.

- There were three phases of discrimination against Jews. Firstly, from 1933 to 1934, they were forbidden from working government jobs, and their businesses were boycotted. Secondly, from 1935 to 1936, the Nuremberg Laws came into effect, and Jews were stripped of their citizenship. Thirdly, from 1937 to 1939, Jews had their property confiscated and were forced to live in ghettos.

- The use of early concentration camps was for three reasons. Namely, to incarcerate enemies of the state, to use inmates as slave labor, and to kill inmates away from the public eye. There were many different types of camps, such as forced labor and prisoner-of-war camps. All operated in a similar structure in that a commandant ran the facility and SS guards maintained order.

- Other groups—excluding Jews—were also killed during the Holocaust. Including communists, Roma and Sinti, Jehovah's Witnesses, homosexuals, those suffering from societal problems like homelessness, and disabled individuals.

- "The Final Solution" was the term that Nazis used to refer to their plan of eradicating all Jews from Europe. Nazis established extermination camps where Jews were transported and murdered in gas chambers using the poisonous gas called Zyklon-B. It is estimated that six million Jews were killed during the mass genocide, with the largest extermination camp, Auschwitz, accounting for 1.1 million.

CHAPTER 6:

Major Turning Points of WWII

The circumstances in World War Two were everchanging. Soldiers were fighting on the Eastern and Western fronts, troops made headway into national interiors, oceans were bombarded with battle, and the general idea of who was going to be victorious changed continuously over the months and years the conflict lasted. Some events did not even seem crucial at the time but progressively chipped away at the military power of Germany and the Axis powers. This is true of almost every war. The only day that war stops is when one side agrees they will cease fighting. The key to this is a systematic and strategic offensive so that small cracks develop in the enemy's morale and military force. All these cracks accumulate until the enemy is dealt a deafening blow that ends the violence. In the context of World War Two, this blow came during the Battle of Berlin because Germany no longer possessed enough power, weapons, and soldiers to continue. However, in the years leading up to this battle, the Allies made several advancements that turned the tide in their favor. It is impossible to point to one of these as being the sole reason for an

Allied victory. Rather, all of their successes accelerated gradually and ensured Nazi Germany's rightful defeat. Some of these turning points stand out and serve as momentous examples of Allied courage and determination. We'll be taking a look at three decisive moments that left Nazi leaders scratching their heads!

The Battle of Britain

Although the Battle of Britain was defensive in nature, the consequences of a British victory were an important element that turned the tide of World War Two. It was the first time that Germany was defeated, leading to a loss of national morale and a stab to the confidence they developed by annexing European countries successfully before 1941. When France fell to the Nazis in June 1940, Hitler was convinced that Britain would seek a peace treaty so as to protect itself from a similar invasion. To his surprise, the English continued fighting. As always, Hitler responded with his Blitzkrieg strategy, this time eyeing British lands. The Nazis called it "Operation Sealion" and were to follow the strategy that has been fruitful for German invasions thus far. Their first step: an air attack. Unbeknownst to Hitler, this was to be their last step as well! The superior Luftwaffe was to fight with the British Royal Air Force (RAF), and the former was convinced that they would be victorious. The RAF was not known to be particularly effective and saw slow growth after World War One, making the Luftwaffe even more confident. Although the Luftwaffe suffered some losses during the Battle of France, by July 10, 1940, three German air fleets were ready for a British attack. Before the battle commenced, Prime Minister Churchill delivered an address. "Upon this battle depends the survival of Christian civilization. Upon it depends our own British life and the long continuity of our institutions and our Empire" (Tucker, 2013, p. 230). Perhaps it was this speech that emboldened the British air force to fight until the end. Germany did not expect the strong defense network that they would be facing. The British Dowding System was a highly unified form of defense that included technology such as radar, fighter aircraft, and ground defenses. Moreover, British defense was divided into four geographical sectors, all of which were equipped with operation rooms, standby pilots, and constant communication with Fighter Command Headquarters.

Formation of Hawker Hurricanes of RAF Fighter Command on patrol defending against Nazi Germany bombers, 1940

Britain's superior radar network let them clearly see where the Germans were attacking from. The German offensive firstly—from July to October—focused on bombing coastal targets so as to cut off shipping operations. On August 13, the Luftwaffe set its sights inland so that it could bomb communication centers and airfields, with the goal of reducing the RAF fleet and causing confusion. Their focus was on the RAF Fighter Command, a type of specialized war aircraft. The

Germans were able to damage Fighter Command, but most of these withstood their attacks and remained operational. August 31 proved to be one of the most devastating days for Fighter Command because the Germans were able to bomb many strategic airfields. That being said, the Nazis underestimated the Brits' ability to recover. As Hitler thought that the enemy air force was sufficiently destroyed, he ordered the Luftwaffe to target England's capital city, London. On September 7, they arrived in the city and started bombing. Although this led to civilian destruction, it allowed Fighter Command to recover and plan an offensive. On September 15, the RAF—stronger than ever— successfully repelled the Luftwaffe from the airspace of London. Suffering severe losses, the Germans continued fighting for a few weeks but were eventually forced to turn around and "postpone" the invasion of Britain. The loss of 1,887 German aircraft was mortifying for Luftwaffe commanders, who quickly questioned their superiority complex (Correll, 2008). Upon winning the battle, Churchill said, "Never in the field of human conflict was so much owed by so many to so few [alluding to the RAF]" (Wiersbe, 1994, p. 60). Not winning this battle left a stain on the Luftwaffe and their future efforts. Additionally, the fact that Britain stayed independent of Nazi tyranny meant a lot in the long run. The launch of the final Allied offensive was done from British shores. Without the heroism and determination of the RAF, Britain might have fallen, and the Luftwaffe would not have suffered the devastation that contributed to the Nazi defeat in 1945. From reading this, we can see the impact of turning points even as early as a year into war. It was one of the first cracks that would see the Nazi machine come falling down!

RAF fighter pilots "scramble" during the Battle of Britain, 1940

Operation Barbarossa

People often mistakenly see the Battle of Stalingrad as a part of Operation Barbarossa because both refer to a German invasion of the Soviet Union. In fact, Operation Barbarossa refers to the German attack on Moscow and the Soviet territory of modern-day Ukraine. It began before the Battle of Stalingrad, and it lasted from June 1941 to December 1941. Although the Battle of Stalingrad was a turning point in itself, the failure of Operation Barbarossa was more influential in changing the tide of the war as it was the first time the Soviets defeated the Nazis. Long before the war started, Hitler set his eyes on the Soviet Union. He despised the communist Stalin and wrongfully believed that the Russian people would welcome any nation that would assist in his removal. Before Hitler introduced Operation Barbarossa, he said, "We have only to kick in the front door and the whole rotten edifice will come tumbling down" (Norris, 2020, p. 148). Hitler further believed that ethnic Russians were inferior and did not have the strength to withstand Germany's Blitzkrieg strategies. Even though Hitler was warned by his military advisors, he ordered the invasion of the Soviet Union that took place on June 22, 1941, with about 3 million German troops crossing the Soviet border (History.com Editors, 2009c). At first, it looked like the invasion was going to be successful because Stalin did not expect an invasion, and German troops took many Soviet troops prisoner, all the while killing Soviet Jews in various towns. German troops went on a rampage whereby they killed commanders and prisoners of war and violated all international war protocols. These actions certainly infuriated Russians, who were increasingly emboldened by Stalin's calls to protect "Mother Russia." In September 1941, the Germans were successful in capturing the territory of Ukraine. Hitler soon placed his attention on the city of Leningrad, but German troops were unable to capture it. In response, the Nazis opted to lock Soviet troops within the city and starve them into submission. To their surprise, Soviet troops did not give up and continued to fight back until they won 872 days later!

That being said, while Leningrad was under siege, German troops made their way to the Soviet capital, Moscow, in October 1941. Hitler called this effort Operation Typhoon and planned that a fall of their capital would signify the end of the Soviet Union. However, the time Germans spent in Leningrad gave Soviet troops time to prepare, and an estimated one million troops were waiting for the Nazis to arrive (History. com Editors, 2009c). After intense fighting, the Germans made their final attempt to encircle and capture the city in November. Yet, after a month of fighting, the strength and resolve of the Soviet troops were too much for German troops. The Soviets pushed Germans out of the city and forced them to retreat! Operation Barbarossa ultimately failed because the Nazis were unable to force the

Soviet Union to accept defeat. Soviet troops and citizens fought together to protect their nation, and although Germans made some territorial advances, Hitler was no closer to reaching his goal of annexing the Soviet Union. A further reason for its characterization as a turning point is that it led to the formation of the Eastern Front. Before the invasion of the Soviet Union, the Germans were solely focused on fighting on the Western Front. But after antagonizing the Soviets, they had to send weapons and troops to the east, which diminished many of their resources. World War Two was now a conflict that needed to be fought on both sides of the European continent. Even so, once the Soviet Union was attacked, they became instrumental in the worldwide war effort and rapidly increased their military capacity. It, therefore, signified the start of Germany against the world, which would eventually lead to its downfall.

A column of Nazi Germany armoured forces during Operation Barbarossa (1941)

The Battle of Normandy

The Battle of Normandy—also called D-day—was a significant turning point in World War Two because it opened the door to a full-scale European invasion by the Allies. The active battle started on June 6, 1944, but months went into planning the invasion. The Allies used deception to their benefit and thought of ways to catch German soldiers off guard. Nazi commanders knew that the Allies were planning a European invasion in order to free France, but they did not know how the invasion was going to play out or where it would take place. This confusion was used by the Allies so that they could ensure entry into France with minimal military casualties and a greater shot at victory. They called their deception strategy Operation Fortitude, with the aim of tricking the Germans regarding where the Allied troops were going to land. Through fake communications, they made the German military believe that they were going to invade a section of France called Pas de Calais. Naturally, German forces were ordered to go to that region and wait for battle. The deception was so intricate that the earlier mentioned General George Patton was stationed in southeast England, where dummy tanks and army ships were placed! The Luftwaffe could only observe it from a distance and thought the weapons were real. In response, the German Wehrmacht patiently waited at Pas de Calais waiting to defend Nazi rule of France. Additionally, the Allies thought it best to attack the Germans by air first. They amassed soldiers and weapons in Britain and gradually began to bomb German territories in France. The Allies destroyed strategic areas used by the Nazis, such as bridges, railroads, and airfields. Therefore, German troops had far fewer weapons and lower morale than they sorely needed to be successful in the anticipated battle. On June 6, all the Allied preparation finally paid off.

American troops approaching Omaha Beach on Normandy Beach, D-Day, 1944

Allied troops under the leadership of General Dwight D. Eisenhower—who later became an American President—attacked through the French beaches of Normandy. That being said, the attack was almost canceled due to bad weather. Because the attack was to start when it was still dark, General Eisenhower wanted clear skies, a full moon, and calm seas. On June 6, the weather was mainly overcast and made it more difficult for troops to navigate the area effectively. Yet, he realized the importance of the day and eventually agreed that they should attack. Perhaps he was thinking that the Germans would be even less prepared as they would not expect the Allies to invade when the weather was bad! When thinking about the actual invasion, you might think that it all happened at once. In fact, there were several stages that ensured an Allied victory. The first step consisted of Allied paratroopers who parachuted behind enemy lines in the early hours of the morning. They were tasked with destroying German targets and taking control of bridges the Allies would need to move into the interior of France. The second step commenced when Allied planes dropped bombs on German troops and defenses along the beaches, and warships started bombing from the sea. To make matters worse for the Nazis, members of the French Resistance cut telephone lines so that German commanders and troops couldn't communicate! The Allies also used dummy soldiers they dropped from the skies so that the enemy did not know who posed a threat. It was only then that the third step took place. Namely, a land invasion of the Normandy beaches. About 6,000 ships landed on the shores, all of which were equipped with tanks, troops, and weapons (*D-Day*, 2018). The Utah and Omaha beaches in Normandy were the main ones the Allied troops used to get entry to the interior. Although American troops were successful in capturing both, the battle at Omaha was particularly brutal, and many American troops lost their lives there. No one really knows how many people were killed during the invasion, but it is clear that the Allies captured about 200,000 German troops and imprisoned them in war camps (Roos, 2019). Moreover, the Allied victory ensured that 150,000 Allied troops—mainly from America, Britain, and Canada—entered French territory. By June 17, this number had grown to 500,000 (*D-Day*, 2018)! D-Day, therefore, allowed for Allied entry into Europe and placed them in a great position for going on the offensive. It was a turning point because now the Allies were settled in German territories with no plans of leaving until the Nazis were driven out. It was the beginning of the end of the Nazi's dream of European domination.

The D-Day Invasion of Normandy, 1944

The Story of Bill Sisk

A witness and participant in the D-Day invasion was the 17-year-old American teenager Herbert Sisk. When he was younger, his family and friends called him "Billy" or "Bill," a nickname his fellow troops also preferred. When World War Two started in 1939, Bill was still in high school and was not that worried about America's involvement in the conflict. He confessed that he did not concern himself with the matter, but that all changed after the Japanese Attack on Pearl Harbor. In response to this attack, and the dangers he would face, he remembered, "I don't think we did much thinking at all" (AFP, 2019). Bill and his friends refused to think about threats to their lives and only wanted to protect their country from further attacks. When he was 16 in 1943, he lied about his age to sign up for the Army. After nine weeks of military training at an Army facility in North Carolina, he joined 15,000 other American troops to cross the U-boat-infested Atlantic Ocean. In Scotland, Bill trained as a radio operator so that he could assist in communication between Allied commanders and troops. He said, "Day after day, we'd go out and practice and come in, practice and come in. One day we went out and then did not come back" (AFP, 2019). Unbeknownst to him, his commanders were so impressed with his progress that he was sent to assist in the Normandy invasion!

Fortunately, he was sent after the battle had lessened in intensity so that he could set up Allied radio lines on shore. With a big radio set on his back, he sailed with older troops to the Utah beach. He remembered that another soldier, wielding a machine gun, told him to move away so that the radio set did not attract attention from the enemy. Bill also remembered the many dead bodies that lay strewn on the beach and how he forced himself to look away. Perhaps empathizing with the scared 17-year-old boy, an older sergeant took him under his wing and treated Bill "like a son" (AFP, 2019). Three days after their arrival—on Bill's 18th birthday—the Allied troops went deeper into the interior of France. A few days later, just as Bill sat down to eat breakfast, he was shot in the leg by a German sniper! He recovered in England but was sent to Germany when the war neared its end. As his battalion advanced on the German city of Frankfurt, Bill was instrumental in the liberation of a concentration camp. There, he saw the horrors of Nazi human rights abuses and, in his advanced years, still had trouble facing what he witnessed. Asked about his experience in the concentration camp, he only said, "You grow up real fast" (AFP, 2019). After the war, Bill returned to the United States, where he finished school and obtained a degree in economics. During his life, he worked at a chain of large stores, built his own home, got married, and had two children. He passed away at the tender age of 96 in 2021. Bill's story teaches us that teenagers have the ability to make a difference and fight for what is right. All we can say is thank you, Bill, and all the veterans who have risked their lives for freedom!

Key Takeaways

- There were many turning points during World War Two. However, a few of these stand out because they changed the trajectory of the conflict on a mass scale.

- The Battle of Britain in 1940 was a turning point because it was the first time Germans were defeated by a European country, many Nazi aircraft were destroyed, and the failure to capture British territory from which the final Allied Offensive was conducted in 1945.

- Operation Barbarossa in 1941 was a turning point because Germans lost many troops during the conflict, the Soviet Union became instrumental in the worldwide Allied war efforts, and it created the Eastern Front that was much more brutal—and required more German weapons and troops—than the Western Front.

- The Battle of Normandy in 1944 was a turning point because it was the beginning of the end. It introduced many Allied troops into continental Europe who fought with Germany from within their annexed territories. It, therefore, changed German goals from offense to defense.

CHAPTER 7:

Victory!

As THE WAR WAS COMING TO A CLOSE, THE BRITISH AUTHOR H.G. Wells wrote, "If we don't end the war, the war will end us" (Ouis, 2020, p. 686). By this, he meant that the Allied powers should not get too comfortable as they made advances on the enemy. Although they were winning by all accounts, the German troops and civilians were still holding onto their dream of victory. Allied leaders knew that the Nazis were not going to accept defeat and would fight to the death as Hitler expected of them. Throughout the war, German propaganda was operating at full force, and many German civilians were scared of what was to happen should their nation lose. When Soviet and other Allied troops went deeper into German territory on their way to Berlin in April 1945, Nazi leaders became aware that their defeat was imminent. It seemed like the only person who still thought that Germany could win was Adolf Hitler. He attempted to stay "loyal" to his people by choosing death rather than submission. Citizens of the Allied nations were eager to see the end of the war and could not wait until the final blow was dealt to the nation that terrorized the world for the prior six years. Let's look at the events that characterized the end of World War Two and a long-awaited Allied victory!

Hitler in the Bunker

Throughout the war, Hitler spent very little time in his main office in Berlin. He opted to stay in his villa in the Bavarian Alps as he ordered the killing of millions of people. Hitler was completely removed from the suffering his war caused and the difficulties he brought upon the German people. It was only on January 16, 1945, that he left his villa and moved to a bunker that was built 55 feet under the chancellery in Berlin. By January, the Allies had begun to bomb areas close to his villa, and it was thought that he would be safe in his 18-roomed secure shelter below Berlin. He would stay there for a total of 105 days, only periodically surfacing for fresh air when they weren't under threat of bombs. With him was his partner, Eva Braun, and his beloved dog, Blondi. Most of his time in the bunker was spent ordering senior Nazi officials to his underground office and strategizing battle tactics with the hope that Germany still had a chance of victory. Nazi officials and commanders routinely visited Hitler and were afraid to tell him that they had lost certain battles and made territorial retreats. The Minister of Propaganda, Joseph Goebbels, moved into the bunker with his family and fueled Hitler's hopes of changing the tide of the war in their favor. When the Soviet Army made advances into Germany, Nazi officials suggested that Hitler and Goebbels leave the facility, but Hitler refused. He believed that Germany still had a chance, and if they were going to lose, he did not want to face the punishment he deserved.

His hopes were crushed on April 22, 1945, when he learned that German troops did not defend the region of Eberswalde and advanced on Berlin. Hitler was furious and reprimanded his officials for supposedly disobeying his orders. During his rant, he yelled, "The armed forces have lied to me, and now the SS has left me in the lurch. The German people have not fought heroically. It deserves to perish" (Swinford, 2012)! Hitler's secretary, Traudl Junge, remembered that he looked like a broken man with all his dreams crushed at once. It was then that he realized suicide was the only option. He heard the bombs going off in Berlin and knew that there was no way out. After discussing his decision with Eva Braun, the pair got married in the bunker in the hope that they would spend eternity together. Additionally, Goebbels and his family stayed loyal to Hitler until the end and prepared for their own deaths. On April 29, Hitler shot himself and his dog and administered a cyanide capsule to his wife. Goebbels's wife, Magda, killed all their children with cyanide, whereafter the pair also shot themselves. Several other Nazi officials in the bunker also ended their lives after Hitler's self-inflicted gunshot was heard throughout the building. Hitler's delusion is clear in his last political statement that he wrote on that day. "After six years of war, which in spite of all setbacks, will go down one day in history as the most glorious and valiant demonstration of a nation's life purpose" (Rosenberg, 2019). The moment Hitler died, the entire world knew that Nazism would soon fall as the instigator of the conflict was removed.

Germany's Agony

Nevertheless, before Hitler died, greater Germany was in a perilous state. Nazi officials were in secret talks when it became clear that a defeat was imminent. They tried to come up with ways that Germany could be saved from the total destruction that Hitler was leading them to. When Hitler ordered troops to attack and defend certain Allied positions, they knew it was nothing but a suicide mission as German forces had no chance of success. The six years of war had depleted Nazi weapons, morale, and the number of active troops in the

Wehrmacht. Commanders were afraid that Hitler would order their execution if they disobeyed what he wanted, while at the same time being aware that their troops had no chance of victory in any of the offenses Hitler expected. This was evident in the Battle of Berlin when Soviet forces finally reached the capital. Nazi troops were stationed all over the city but were immediately crushed when the superior Soviet weapons arrived. German troops were afraid of each other because they faced the threat of their own execution if they spoke out against Nazi efforts. Similarly, German citizens were lost and confused. Most did not even know about the Holocaust and had been taught to fear the Allied powers, especially the Soviets, who had now rolled into their capital. Perhaps it was this fear that made Berlin citizens bear arms and fight to the death. Other citizens feared the idea of active fighting and opted to hide or commit suicide. It is estimated that 7,000 Germans in Berlin killed themselves when the Soviets approached, and the town of Demmin saw more than 1,000 suicides in 72 hours (Reimann, 2016).

Many government officials, parents, children, and senior citizens died together because they dreaded what the Allies would do to them. The Nazi government distributed flyers to the public that outlined ways in which they could kill themselves. Sadly, some of these fears were realized when Soviet forces committed acts of rape and murder on ordinary civilians once they arrived. From 1940, German cities and towns were routinely bombed, and by 1945, about 4.8 million homes were laid in rubble (Jacobs, 2023). Many Germans, therefore, had no way to hide when Allied forces entered their communities. Additionally, many Germans starved to death as there was no food or water readily available. Critical infrastructure in major cities was obliterated, which threatened their survival even before the Allies invaded the ground. As many troops were already killed, Hitler ordered that average civilians had to fight as well. Women, children, and the elderly were recruited and given weapons to defend Nazi ideals. Of course, they had no training and did not stand a chance against the advancing Allied invasion. If they refused, Nazi sympathizers hung them or shot them on the spot. Citizens were now fighting the enemy and their own government, which believed that loyalty was more important than survival. When Hitler died, his successor knew that if Germany was to survive, unconditional surrender was the only option.

Surrender

Before Hitler's death, he had appointed Karl Dönitz to succeed him as chancellor. On May 1, 1945, Dönitz made a speech and stated, "My first task is to save the German people from annihilation by the advancing Bolshevist [Soviet] enemy. The military struggle continues only with this aim" (Frischauer, 1964, p. 223). However, this speech was only given to lessen the news of Hitler's death for those who believed him to be a savior. Dönitz rightfully thought that he could not alienate the public who swore to fight until the end. But deep down, he knew that Germany could not stand more fighting, and the nation would be wiped out if they did not accept defeat. During the week he was in power, the Soviets took control of Berlin, and only a few German territories were still under Nazi authority. Dönitz had no option other than to follow Allied guidance and issue an unconditional surrender that would end the war and bring Nazi rule to an end. On May 7, 1945, Dönitz ordered General Alfred Jodl to head to the French city of Reims, where a surrender document was awaiting him. In the presence of Dwight D. Eisenhower's Chief of Staff and a Soviet general, Jodl signed the document ensuring that all German attacks would stop on May 8, 1945, at 11.01 p.m. Yet, the Soviet Union was not pleased with the document and wanted a German surrender pertaining only to them. Again, Dönitz had no other choice but to order the signing of another surrender agreement. On May 8, German

Commander Wilhelm Keitel signed the document that was handed to him by the earlier mentioned Soviet General Georgi Zhukov in Berlin. This is the reason why "Victory Day" is celebrated on May 9 in Russia, as opposed to May 8 in other European countries. Karl Dönitz knew that the future of Germany was unstable. In his last radio address on the day of surrender, he soberly said, "With the occupation of Germany, the power lies with the occupying powers. It is in their hands whether or not I and the government appointed by me can operate" (Derry & Jarman, 1964, p. 408). They did not know what the future held.

Field Marshall Wilhelm Keitel signs the final surrender terms, Victory in Europe, 1945

World War Two had finally ended in Europe! Street parties were held in the major cities of all the Allied powers, such as Washington, London, Moscow, and Paris. That being said, conflict in the Pacific was still ongoing. Emperor Hirohito of Japan believed that their war goals were separate from those of the Nazis, and just because the Germans surrendered did not mean that his empire should too. Japan continued fighting, and the Americans planned how they would get them to fall, as Germany had. America was already bombing Japanese territory, but President Truman was advised that a land invasion would realize its ultimate goal. Truman was unwilling to send more American troops to Japan and chose to drop an atomic bomb on the country so as to force them into capitulating. On August 6, 1945, American pilots dropped an atomic bomb—nicknamed "Little Boy"—on the Japanese city of Hiroshima. And when Japan still refused to surrender, they dropped another—nicknamed "Fat Man"—on the city of Nagasaki on August 9. Nuclear bombs had never been used before, and the level of destruction was immense. The Japanese death toll from these attacks is estimated to range between 70,000 to 135,000 and 60,000 to 80,000, respectively (History.com Editors, 2009f). On September 2, 1945, Japan finally surrendered, and World War Two was over in its entirety. Liberation from Nazi tyranny had arrived!

Winston Churchill Waves to Crowd After V-E Day, End of War in Europe, 1945

Liberation!

The Allied powers were elated. All their hard work paid off, and their soldiers had not died in vain. Together, they had handed Germany a devastating blow and hoped that the likes of Adolf Hitler would never be seen again. On the day of surrender, American President Harry Truman celebrated by stating, "The Western world has been freed of the evil forces which for five years and longer have imprisoned bodies and broken the lives of millions upon millions of free-born men" (Boyer, 2022, p. 106). The British Prime Minister, Winston Churchill, said, "Finally, almost the whole world was united against the evil-doers, who are now prostrate before us" (Taylor, 2014, p. 98). And the Soviet leader, Josef Stalin, honored the Russian people by saying, "Glory to the heroic Red Army, which upheld the independence of our Motherland and won victory over the enemy" (Edwards, 2018, p. 97)! The citizens of the Allied powers were very grateful to see the end of World War Two and shared in the celebrations instigated by their leaders. Nonetheless, all the mentioned speeches made note of the many deaths it took to realize their goals of victory. Millions of troops and civilians had died during the war, and practically everyone in an Allied country knew someone—or a few—who did not come home. It was truly a bittersweet feeling because the world was free from the horrors of Nazism and the resultant conflict, but it came at a high cost. The celebration was intertwined with mourning, and all the troops who came back from the warzone were scarred from seeing their friends die on the battlefield.

No more was the effect of liberation felt by survivors in the many concentration camps that scattered the European landscape. Some of the concentration camps were liberated before the official surrender of Germany as Allied forces advanced toward Berlin. Yet, freed prisoners were still considered enemies of the state and feared for their lives.

After the surrender, Jews and other incarcerated groups were freed with no fear of punishment. It was only then that the world witnessed the true horrors practiced by the Nazis. Their brutality on the battlefield seemed mild when liberators were met with prisoners that were starving and sick with disease. To Allied forces, these prisoners looked like skeletons who lived among thousands of corpses that the Nazis did not even bother to bury. When the Soviets liberated Auschwitz, they even found 14,000 pounds of human hair (*Liberation of Nazi camps*, 2019)! Sadly, the condition of many prisoners was critical, and thousands died days or weeks after liberation. Sadly, their new status as free citizens did not mean they could go home, as everything they owned was destroyed throughout the war. The Allied powers set up displacement camps that housed many liberated Jews until they could find work or emigrate to family or friends. The psychological trauma that all of these individuals experienced stayed with them forever, as everyone witnessed the death and loss of loved ones. Liberation had come, but their lives were damaged to such an extent that most felt lost and suffered from depression and PTSD. World War Two was over, liberation was tasted, and the whole world waited to see what would happen next.

Allied military personnel in Paris celebrating V-J Day, End of World War II, 1945

The Stories of Mady Gerrard and Hannelore Kohl

Mady Gerrard and Hannelore Kohl were both teenagers when liberation came to Europe. The two girls had vastly different experiences during the war, as Mady was a Hungarian Jew, and Hannelore was considered an "Aryan" German. By reading their stories, you will recognize that in war, there are no winners, and oftentimes it is the most vulnerable among us that are hit the hardest. Mady Gerrard was only 14 years old when her native Hungary was invaded by the Nazis in March 1944. Her family had heard about the horrors that Jews faced when they fell under German rule, and because the war was coming to a close, they knew that the only reason for an invasion was to get rid of European Jews living there. She did not hide with her family, and all of them were taken to Auschwitz on July 8. Mady thankfully survived the selection process and was tasked with sorting luggage until she was sent to another concentration camp. Concerning the new camp, she remembered, "Compared to Auschwitz, it was paradise because they didn't kill us, and we didn't have the stench of the burning bodies" (*Mady Gerrard*, 2022). Yet, it was not to be. A while later, she was sent to Bergen–Belsen in January 1945. She said, "There was no sanitation, no showers. We were put into barracks, with no furniture, lying on the floor with very little food" (*Mady Gerrard*, 2022). Mady experienced death on a scale she never thought she would. One instance stood out to her; when her best friend— riddled with lice—died in her arms from starvation. The liberation of Bergen–Belsen came on April 15, 1945. Mady sat in her barrack when they heard a jeep arriving. It was a British soldier! She recalled that he was shocked seeing her and other girls who, by this point, resembled skeletons. The soldier went back to his jeep and retrieved a dose of delousing powder that he sprayed on the girls. Mady remembered, "All the lice and fleas dropped dead on the floor; it looked like we'd had a carpet full of lice fitted the way they now covered the floor" (*Mady Gerrard*, 2022). She was sent to Sweden to recuperate, and after a stint in Hungary, she immigrated to Britain, where she eventually established a fashion brand and built herself up financially. Sadly, her father and boyfriend were lost in the war. When asked about liberation, she claimed, "It must've been the best day of my life" (*Mady Gerrard*, 2022)!

Hannelore Kohl had a different experience during Nazi rule as she was considered the perfect German. In fact, she was born in 1933 and grew up knowing nothing else than a life dictated by Hitler's whims. At first, she continued going to school and was not bothered by war. However, when Germany started losing, her life changed rapidly.

Hannelore witnessed regular bombings and the fear associated with them. In 1945, German schools were closed, and no one knew what to expect once they accepted defeat. She was only 12 years old when the Soviets marched on Berlin and invaded the areas surrounding it. She was told that the Soviets were brutal, and it would be better to die, but her mother did not have the courage to follow through. In May, she experienced their brutality by enduring the worst moment of her life. Hannelore and her mother were raped by Soviet soldiers who were emboldened by their victory. She remembered, "I was dumped like a sack of potatoes out of the first floor [when they were finished]" (Mail Online, 2011). For the rest of her life, she was traumatized by this experience and is said to have been triggered by the "smell of male sweat, garlic, alcohol and even the sound of spoken Russian" (Mail Online, 2011). After the war, she lived in Allied-occupied Germany and became engaged to the future Chancellor of Germany, Helmut Kohl. Unfortunately, her trauma, in addition to an antibiotic-induced allergy to sunlight, led to her committing suicide at the age of 68 in 2001.

Both these stories are tragic and prove that teenagers and children from the Allied and Axis powers suffered through no fault of their own. World War Two brought about immeasurable suffering for everyone involved, and it is important to recognize the horrors experienced by all sides of the conflict.

Key Takeaways

- During the last phase of the war, Adolf Hitler stayed in a secure bunker below Berlin, dictating orders from there. He was increasingly delusional and thought that Germany could still be victorious. When it became clear that they had lost, Hitler committed suicide on April 29, 1945.

- German citizens were in an agonizing situation because their homes were bombed, there was not enough food and water, and thousands of their fellow countrymen died during the battle. When the Soviets approached, many chose to fight, commit suicide, or hide from the enemy.

- After Hitler's death, Karl Dönitz became chancellor of Germany and knew that they had to surrender. On May 7, 1945, Germany signed a document of surrender, ending the conflict. On May 8, 1945, Germany signed another document surrendering to the Soviet Union. Japan only surrendered on September 2, 1945, after America dropped two atomic bombs on Hiroshima and Nagasaki.

- The Allied powers celebrated, but it was bittersweet as many of their citizens had died. It was only when they liberated concentration camps that the Holocaust came to light, and the world learned the extent of Nazi horrors.

CHAPTER 8:

The Aftermath of Bloodshed

ALTHOUGH LIBERATION AND AN ALLIED VICTORY WERE good news, the world now faced the aftermath of World War Two. The whole world was grappling with how Europe should move forward. Leaders asked questions such as: What should be done to help the Holocaust survivors? Who will lead Germany after the downfall of Nazism? And how should the enemy be punished? Many of these questions were discussed at the Yalta and Potsdam Conferences by leaders from the United States, Britain, and the Soviet Union from February 4 to February 11 and July 17 to August 2, 1945, respectively. There were some disagreements—especially between the Soviet Union and America—but they agreed on five broad goals. It became known as the five D's. Namely, demilitarization, denazification, democratization, decentralization, and deindustrialization. Under each of these headers were several immediate actions to be undertaken so that the region was stabilized and any further conflict was prevented. It was a very difficult task because most of Europe and Eastern Asia lay in ruins, and several countries had no set borders anymore. The entire continent had to be restructured, and their economies had to be built up from scratch. More so, the scale of death and trauma left practically all Europeans in a state of despair. The future was definitely going to be difficult!

Immediate Aftermath

As soon as the war ended, Germany was split up into four zones. Western Germany was carved into sections controlled by the United States, Great Britain, and France. Eastern Germany was given to the Soviet Union under the agreement that all the Allied powers were working together toward German self-governance in the future. Berlin was an important economic spot deep in the interior that was now controlled by the Soviets. Therefore, it was agreed to carve Berlin up with the eastern part going to the Soviet Union and the western part going to the other three. In the Pacific, America took control of Japan, and the Allied powers split Korea—who supported the Japanese war effort—into two, with the Soviet Union controlling the north and the others controlling the south. In Europe, Karl Dönitz and other former Nazi officials had no say in governance because they were all viewed as criminals. Instead, Nazi leaders and other prominent individuals were tried for their actions during the war and had to face punishment for their heinous deeds. There were several war trials, such as one focusing solely on doctors who operated in concentration camps and a number of trials bringing SS guards to justice. The most prominent trial, however, took place in Nuremberg, where the top Nazi leaders were held accountable. The Soviet Union was not happy with the decision and wanted to execute them immediately. But the other Allied powers felt that they should be treated like humans and do the opposite of the Nazis by showing them mercy through a civilized trial. The basis of the trial was that Nazi leaders broke the rules of war as agreed in the

Geneva Convention. The defendants also committed crimes against humanity through their implementation of the Holocaust, the use of slave labor, and torture. The Nuremberg Trial lasted until October 1946 and shone a spotlight on all the evils committed by Germany's top Nazis.

The Accused, Nuremberg trial, 1945-46

The 19 defendants were questioned, and the world came to know the extent of their terrible acts. Most of them were executed, but some received jail time, and others—like the President of the Central Bank, Hjalmar Schacht—were acquitted. Figures such as the former President of the Reichstag Hermann Göring shocked the world when he continued his anti-Semitic stance from the stand, saying, "In Berlin, Jews controlled almost one hundred percent of the theaters and cinemas before the rise to power" (Goldensohn, 2010, p. 107). Göring committed suicide by ingesting cyanide only hours before his scheduled execution. That being said, the immediate aftermath for lesser-known Nazis, like the soldiers who were caught by Allied powers, was far less high profile, with most not afforded the luxury of a courtroom. Axis soldiers were kept in prisoner camps by the Soviets all over Germany, and there are accounts of many German civilians being killed or raped by Soviet soldiers during this period. Additionally, hundreds of thousands of Jews were taken to replacement camps where they were to embark on their new "liberated" lives. All of them lost everything they owned and had to find a way out of these camps to build their lives anew. Many Jews even faced further discrimination if they moved east because the Soviets—many anti-Semitic themselves—took control of the many regions in Eastern Europe previously controlled by the Nazis. Countries like Poland, Hungary, Romania, and Czechoslovakia were all blended into the Soviet Union and had no military capacity to fight against it. For those individuals still living in Germany, life was no better. They had no freedom of self-governance, most of their cities and towns were destroyed, and practically everyone lost loved ones during the conflict.

The economic situation across Europe was dire because most industries were shut down, and their currencies were of no value. Moreover, it was impossible to be innovative and active citizens because the infrastructure was destroyed with no finances to stimulate growth. The American response to this came in the form of financial aid, called the Marshall Plan. The United States started this in 1947 with the goal of building up European democracies, with a focus on Germany, so that they did not fall into economic trouble, which America realized was one of the reasons for the rise of Nazism in the first place! About 5% of America's Gross Domestic Product (GDP) went to Europe until it was thought that their economies were sufficiently developed to operate on their own in 1951 (History.com Editors, 2009b). Although the investment in Europe was certainly to help countries ravaged by war because it was "not directed against any country, but against hunger, poverty, desperation, and chaos," it was also a diplomatic decision on the part of the United States (History.com Editors, 2009b). As mentioned, the Soviet Union took control of much of Eastern Europe and did not appear favorable toward self-governance in East Germany. In fact, when the Marshall Plan was discussed, Soviet officials did not even attend the meeting. The threat to the West was no longer Nazism but communism as practiced by Josef Stalin. Strong European national economies were thought to be the only repellent to further Soviet advancements to the West. By all accounts, the Marshall Plan was very effective, and Germany—in addition to other American allies—recovered quickly. By 1952, all the nations that received aid exhibited stronger economic growth than what they had at the start of the war, and in 1949, Western Germany was allowed to hold elections and choose their representatives. Sadly, another conflict grew as a direct result of the gains the Soviet Union made during and after World War Two. The world was now to witness the Cold War until 1989.

Long-Term Effects

The Cold War got its name because it never actually developed into a full-blown worldwide conflict. Yet, it was still a difficult period for many countries living under the threat of possible annihilation by atomic bombs and further caused the outbreak of several proxy wars around the globe. All this started when the Soviets, who controlled East Germany and East Berlin, did not want to give up the territory and formed an alliance with German communists living there. In 1949, the Soviets established the German Democratic Republic, and the other former Allied powers established West Germany, officially called the Federal Republic of Germany. Even before World War Two,

Western democracies were weary of the Soviet Union, but the aftermath of the war ensured that the Soviets now moved closer to countries like Great Britain and France. In 1955, the Soviet Union and Eastern European countries formed a military alliance known as the Warsaw Pact in response to the North Atlantic Treaty Organization (NATO), an American-led military alliance of worldwide democracies that was formed in 1949. The hostility between democratic and communist countries was in the making, and postwar Germany became the symbol of this division. The British Prime Minister, Winston Churchill, said, "An iron curtain has descended across the [European] continent" (Kearns, 2009, p. 155). The Soviets did not allow the Allied powers to fly over their new territory or be involved in the functioning of the region. The pinnacle of the hostility in Germany came in 1961 when the Soviets ordered a 12-foot concrete wall to be built in their sector of Berlin to stop anyone from leaving. The iron curtain that Churchill spoke about was now a literal wall that kept the different ideologies apart! The greater the influence of the Soviet Union, the greater the anxieties of Western countries. America became involved in many wars around the world in an attempt to stop the communist ideology from spreading. One notable example was the Vietnam War, which lasted from 1955 to 1975, when the Americans wanted to stop the spread of the Soviet-supported VietCong Party, which wanted to make Vietnam a communist country. Furthermore, the spread of communism influenced the Chinese Revolution in 1949, making it a one-party state, and the Soviet Union was instrumental in establishing North Korea, which still follows Stalin's ideology in modern times.

During the years of the Cold War, many African countries became independent as well. This was also due to the aftermath of World War Two, as many of the African soldiers who fought on behalf of the Allied powers were emboldened by the values of freedom and liberation. In the 1960s, 17 African countries gained independence from European countries that were under their authority. World War Two had left most European nations with much less power and economic strength, which made it difficult to hold onto their colonies. Related to this was the founding of the United Nations (UN). The UN was established in 1945 in the aftermath of the war so that different nations could come together and sort out their disagreements in a diplomatic manner. In plain terms, it was set up because Allied leaders thought that an institution that encourages dialogue could lessen hostilities before World War Three could erupt. A pillar on which the UN stands is human rights, and as more countries joined, it became clear that colonization did not afford African countries the human right of self-governance. Additionally, the UN played a large part in the creation of Israel in 1948. Before World War Two, Palestine was under the authority of Great Britain, but after the war, they realized that Jewish individuals had nowhere to call home. They believed that if Jews were given a country, they would be safer in the face of anti-Semitism. Thousands of Jews moved to the area, and Israel still offers citizenship to anyone with Jewish heritage today! Unfortunately, since Israel's founding, there has been conflict between Israelis and Palestinians in the region, as both believe they have right over the land. The UN tried to address this in 1947 when they carved the nation up, with each group getting a section of the region, but it remains a divisive issue to this day.

The aftermath of World War Two also catapulted the United States into becoming a superpower. Throughout the conflict, many American jobs were created in wartime production, and many previously marginalized groups—such as women and black individuals—entered the workforce to supplement the men on the battlefield. When the war ended, American soldiers returned home, and the workforce was larger than ever. This led to extensive economic growth and the Gross National Product (GNP) rising from $300 billion in 1950 to $500 billion in 1960 (Pruitt, 2020). There was also more social cohesion due to the country's united fight against communism. These factors induced a united American public who were focused on national progress. As the war and its aftereffects led to a decline of Great Britain, America, therefore, became the richest Western nation. Moreover, America's role in the reconstruction efforts after the war left them with great global influence that they continue to enjoy to this day. The United States grew to become so influential that they were instrumental in the fall of communism, leading to the removal of the Berlin Wall in 1989 and the reunification of Germany in 1990! The most important long-term effect takes a more somber tone. Namely, the emotional trauma it left on survivors and the impact it had on future generations. Millions of future generations will never be born due to the Holocaust and deaths on the battlefield. Regrettably, we will never know how many future lives were lost during the tragedy. The number of those who survived World War Two and the Holocaust reduces every year, which is why it is so essential that we read about their lives and learn from their stories. That way, we can all work together to make sure that something like World War Two never happens again.

Do your best to respect and be kind to everyone, irrespective of whether you look or think the same. Every human being is unique, and now you know what can happen if a large swath of people devalues others. World War Two serves as a great example of what we should never allow in modern times. Think about all the people you read about, and be a hero in your own life!

The Story of Benjamin Ferencz

A man who saw the Nuremberg trials play out before his eyes was the Jewish–American lawyer Benjamin Ferencz. In fact, he was the youngest prosecutor who saw Nazi commanders face justice at the tender age of 27. Benjamin was born in Romania in 1920, but his Jewish family immigrated to the United States when he was a baby. His parents were escaping rampant anti-Semitism and thought that their new son would have more chances of success in the "land of opportunity." History proved them right! He grew up in New York and went to Harvard Law School after graduating high school. Seeing that his country needed soldiers when America entered World War Two, he enlisted in the United States Army, which took him to France, where he participated in the Battle of Normandy. After the war ended, Benjamin put on his lawyer hat and was tasked with investigating Nazi war crimes. His new job required him to visit concentration camps and gather evidence of their horrors. He said, "There is no doubt I was indelibly traumatized by my experiences as a war crimes investigator of Nazi extermination centers. I still try not to talk or think about the details" (The Associated Press, 2023). Upon thinking about the details, he remembered the bodies of Holocaust victims "piled up like cordwood" (The Associated Press, 2023). Benjamin was even sent to Hitler's former villa, where he looked for incriminating evidence! A while after, he was honorably discharged and headed back to New York to practice law. But it was not to be. His superiors wanted him to prosecute Nazi war criminals, and after getting married to his childhood sweetheart, Gertrude, he headed back to Germany.

Once there, he headed a team of prosecutors in a case of Nazi commanders responsible for the deaths of more than one million Jews. He impressed the court because he favored using German writings as opposed to witnesses to present his case. His success was clear in that all the commanders under trial were convicted, and half of them were executed. Years later, Benjamin said, "When the long judgment was read, I felt vindicated. Our pleas to protect humanity by the rule of law had been upheld" (The Associated Press, 2023). Nonetheless, this was not the end of his journey in Germany. His case was successfully completed, and Benjamin got to work helping several Holocaust survivors by legally returning their property, religious items, and business that the Nazis had stolen from them. Similarly, he also spearheaded lawsuits that made sure that Nazi victims were financially compensated for their losses and the psychological trauma they suffered under Nazi rule. After he was satisfied with doing all he could, he returned to the United States, where he practiced law and started a family, having four children. Throughout the rest of his life, he was involved in several Jewish and humanitarian organizations by focusing on the legal aspect of their troubles. His beloved Gertrude passed away in 2019, and Benjamin died in 2023 at the age of 103. A full life that undoubtedly brought positive change!

Key Takeaways

- After World War Two, Germany and Japan were occupied by the Allied powers. Germany and the capital of Berlin were split up into four sectors where the Soviet Union controlled the east, and the United States, France, and Great Britain controlled the west.

- The Soviet Union took control of several Eastern European countries, thereby giving credence to communism. Nazi criminals were tried during war crime trials, with the most influential being the Nuremberg Trials, which tried Nazi's top leaders.

- America assisted in building up Germany and greater Europe by giving them funds through the Marshall Plan.

- The long-term effects follow the immediate effects, as the Soviet Union wanted to spread communism. They kept their sector of Germany and Berlin and enforced this with the Berlin Wall. The Cold War erupted, whereby there was a clash of ideologies on the world stage. Churchill called this the "Iron Curtain," which continued until the fall of communism and the dissolution of the Soviet Union in 1989.

- The aftermath of the war also led to the creation of the United Nations and gave rise to an independence movement in Africa after seeing European colonies fall and the establishment of Israel.

- The United States became a superpower due to a thriving postwar economy and an increase in its global influence due to its critical role in World War Two.

CONCLUSION

THE AMERICAN PRESIDENT DWIGHT D. EISENHOWER SAID, "I hate war as only a soldier who has lived it can, only as one who has seen its brutality, its futility, its stupidity" (Thomsett & Thomsett, 2015, p. 54). The start of World War Two was based on Adolf Hitler's warped ideas on race and territorial expansion to try and establish a world full of "Aryan" Germans. Rampant anti-Semitism was cultivated through Nazi propaganda, and a cult of personality surrounding Hitler soon ensued. When he invaded Poland in 1939, the world could no longer ignore the situation and watch the evils espoused by his ideology take over a continent. Although war is certainly a serious and somber undertaking, democracies around the world united to form the Allied powers. Japan and Italy—both with selfish goals of their own—joined Hitler in forming the Axis powers so that they could increase their own global strength. Over a few months, many countries joined each side in the conflict, and the world was engulfed in a humanitarian disaster that led to a level of death and destruction never before witnessed in human history. There were many battles, such as the Battle of France, of Bulge, and of Stalingrad, that killed millions of soldiers and civilians. Each of the participating nations was led by men whose personal lives affected how they handled the war. Emperor Hirohito of Japan was emboldened by his status as a "divine" leader, Mussolini of Italy was a bully who did not allow any dissenting Italian opinions, and Franklin D. Roosevelt was a patriotic American who was not going to sit back after Japan attacked his troops at Pearl Harbor. Additionally, there were several heroic individuals that assisted in turning the tide of the war in the Allies' favor. The American Virginia Hall was instrumental in the French resistance against the Nazis, and the Irish Richard Hayes decoded secret Nazi communications that helped the Allies strategize war offenses, to name only two. Even some German citizens, like Hans and Sophie Scholl, fought the Nazis from within by distributing flyers denouncing Hitler!

As the war progressed, Germany was losing steam. There were many scenarios that proved Hitler's defeat was imminent. During the Battle of Britain, Germany was defeated in the skies; during Operation Barbarossa, Germany was defeated by the Soviets; and during the Battle of Normandy, Allied forces were able to move into the interior of Europe and eventually push the Nazis out. All these efforts forced Germany to surrender in April 1945, which finally brought liberation to the world. That being said, the process of building Europe up from its ruins was difficult, and it gave rise to a greater influence of the Soviet Union, which became a hostile nation, ultimately resulting in the Cold War. The world came to know about the Holocaust, which the Nazis kept largely hidden during their time in power. Allied powers saw the horrors committed against Jewish and other individuals considered "racially inferior." Similarly, it was only after World War Two that the total of those murdered in the Holocaust came to light: six million! Not only that, but the world also had to face the fact that about 60 million soldiers and civilians lost their lives as a direct consequence of the conflict. World War Two will remain a stain on history and serves as an example of what can happen if a country has an evil leader at the helm.

"Never again" is a sentiment you often hear when the topic of discussion is World War Two. However, if we are going to prevent something like it from occurring again, it is up to each of us to respect and love each other. By reading this book, you have certainly learned a lot, but there remains so much more. It is impossible to do justice to all those who lost their lives from 1939 to 1945 in a single book. As you have seen, many children and teenagers were witnesses to the tragedy that was World War Two. Some of them made a significant difference and were instrumental in doing their part to change the trajectory of the conflict. They were no different from you, and you respected them by choosing to learn about the war. Do all you can to encourage your family and friends to follow suit. Remember, you are never too small to make a difference! This was only the start of your journey in learning about the realities of war. Make it your mission to further your research and become a historian in your own right!

APPENDIX:

10 Extraordinary Facts About WWII!

1. During the war, some of Hitler's family members did not support him. His nephew, William Hitler, even served in the United States Navy!

2. Polish troops enlisted a brown bear from Syria as a private in an Army Unit. He was named Wojtek and carried heavy machinery. After the war, he was sent to a British zoo, where he died in 1963.

3. After the United States entered the war, citizens naturally disliked Germany and changed German-sounding words temporarily. Many Americans called hamburgers "liberty steaks!"

4. The Soviet Union suffered the most deaths on the battlefield. In fact, 80% of Russian men born in 1923 were killed during the conflict (Team Mighty, We Are The Mighty, 2015).

5. Many babies were born in concentration camps. A Polish midwife incarcerated in Auschwitz delivered about 3,000 babies during her time there.

6. A Japanese soldier, Hiroo Onoda, never learned that the war ended in 1945. During the conflict, he fled into a Philippine jungle and stayed there until 1974, when his former commander finally found him!

7. Rationing was a part of life for Allied and Axis troops. Every British soldier was given three sheets of toilet paper daily, whereas Americans were given 22 sheets each!

8. When the Allies started to bomb the German capital, their first bomb landed on the only elephant living in the Berlin Zoo.

9. After the United States dropped the atomic bombs on Hiroshima and Nagasaki, they planned to drop a third one on Tokyo if Japan did not surrender.

10. More Soviet troops and civilians died during the Battle of Stalingrad than American and British casualties combined throughout the entire war.

Thank you for reading! If you enjoyed this book, we'd really appreciate it if you could leave a review on Amazon. This will help us to continue to provide great books, and it will help our potential buyers make confident buying decisions. We will be forever grateful – thank you in advance!

REFERENCES

Abbott, C. (2010). *21 speeches that shaped our world: The people and ideas that changed the way we think*. Random House.

Adolf Hitler. (2009, October 29). History. https://www.history.com/topics/world-war-ii/adolf-hitler-1

AFP. (2019, May 15). *At 17, Bill Sisk fought from the shores of Normandy to Germany*. France 24. https://www.france24.com/en/20190515-17-bill-sisk-fought-shores-normandy-germany

Anti-Jewish legislation in prewar Germany. (2019). United States Holocaust Memorial museum. https://encyclopedia.ushmm.org/content/en/article/anti-jewish-legislation-in-prewar-germany

Anti-Semitism Globally. (2005, March 6). *Nazi Germany and anti-Jewish policy*. ADL. https://www.adl.org/resources/backgrounder/nazi-germany-and-anti-jewish-policy

Bali, B. V. K. (2013). *Military wisdom: military wisdom by Brigadier V.K. Bali: Military Wisdom - Insights from a Seasoned Officer*. Prabhat Prakashan.

Battle of Berlin. (2019). Ducksters. https://www.ducksters.com/history/world_war_ii/battle_of_berlin.php

Battle of Bulge: the greatest American battle of the war. (2020, December 17). National Veterans Memorial and Museum. https://nationalvmm.org/battle-of-the-bulge-the-greatest-american-battle-of-the-war/

Battle of the Bulge. (n.d.). U.S. Army. https://www.army.mil/botb/#:~:text=Early%20on%20the%20misty%20winter

The Battle of Dunkirk the start of the war. (n.d.). Twinkle. https://www.christtheking.wirral.sch.uk/serve_file/901005

Battle of France. (2007). Cs.mcgill.ca.
https://www.cs.mcgill.ca/~rwest/wikispeedia/wpcd/wp/b/Battle_
of_France.htm#:~:text=Total%20allied%20losses%20inclu

Battle of Midway. (2019). Ducksters.
https://www.ducksters.com/history/world_war_ii/battle_of_midwa
y.php

Battle of Stalingrad. (2019). Ducksters.
https://www.ducksters.com/history/world_war_ii/battle_of_staling
rad.php

Benford, T. B. (2001). *Pearl Harbor amazing facts.* American Book Publishers.

Benito Mussolini. (n.d.). Encyclopedia.ushmm.org.
https://encyclopedia.ushmm.org/content/en/article/benito-
mussolini-
1#:~:text=In%20May%201939%2C%20Mussolini%20signed

Beyer, G. (2022, July 6). *7 talented generals who shaped World War II.*
TheCollector. https://www.thecollector.com/most-talented-
generals-of-word-war-ii/

Bienaimé, P. (2015, April 14). *Why France's World War II defense failed so
miserably.* Business Insider. https://www.businessinsider.com/the-
story-of-the-maginot-line-2015-4

Biography: George Patton. (2019). Ducksters.com.
https://www.ducksters.com/history/world_war_ii/george_patton.p
hp

Biography: Japanese Emperor Hirohito. (2014). Ducksters.com.
https://www.ducksters.com/history/world_war_ii/hirohito.php

Biography: Joseph Stalin. (2018). Ducksters.com.
https://www.ducksters.com/biography/joseph_stalin.php

Biography: President Franklin D. Roosevelt for kids. (2018). Ducksters.com.
https://www.ducksters.com/biography/uspresidents/franklindroose
velt.php

Biography: Winston Churchill. (2019). Ducksters.com.
https://www.ducksters.com/biography/winston_churchill.php

Boyer, M. G. (2022). *Monthly entries for the spiritual but not religious through the year: texts, reflections, journal/meditations, and prayers for the spiritual but not religious.* Wipf and Stock Publishers.

Budnik, R. (2018, September 6). *The 6-year-old soldier who fought at the Battle of Stalingrad.* Warhistoryonline. https://www.warhistoryonline.com/world-war-ii/youngest-soldier-of-wwii.html?edg-c=1&Exc_D_LessThanPoint002_p1=1

Case, L. C. H. (2013). *Bold beliefs in camouflage: a - z briefings.* FriesenPress.

Chamberlain, N. (2008). *Radio address by Neville Chamberlain, Prime Minister, September 3, 1939.* Avalon.law.yale.edu. https://avalon.law.yale.edu/wwii/gb3.asp#:~:text=Now%20may%20God%20bless%20you

Childers, T. (2021, March 15). *The political upheavals in Germany in 1932.* Wondrium Daily. https://www.wondriumdaily.com/the-political-upheavals-in-germany-in-1932/

Classification system in Nazi concentration camps. (2019). United States Holocaust Memorial Museum. https://encyclopedia.ushmm.org/content/en/article/classification-system-in-nazi-concentration-camps

The Cold War for kids: Berlin Wall. (n.d.). Www.ducksters.com. https://www.ducksters.com/history/cold_war/berlin_wall.php#:~:text=East%20Germany%20became%20a%20communist

Correll, J. T. (2008). *How the Luftwaffe lost the battle of Britain.* Air & Space Forces Magazine. https://www.airandspaceforces.com/article/0808battle/#:~:text=In%20all%2C%20the%20RAF%20lost

D-Day: the invasion of Normandy. (2018). Ducksters.com. https://www.ducksters.com/history/world_war_ii/d-day_invasion_of_normandy.php

D-Day deception: operation fortitude south. (n.d.). English Heritage. https://www.english-heritage.org.uk/visit/places/dover-castle/history-and-stories/d-day-deception/#:~:text=The%20aim%20of%20the%20deception

Derry, T. K., & Jarman, T. L. (1964). *The European world, 1870–1961*. Ungar.

Disabled people. (2019). Holocaust Memorial Day Trust.
    https://www.hmd.org.uk/learn-about-the-holocaust-and-
    genocides/nazi-persecution/disabled-people/

Duo, M. (2015, February 16). *A bucket of balls & backbone like a boss–Trooper
    Stan Scott.* Breach Bang Clear. https://www.breachbangclear.com/a-
    bucket-of-balls-backbone/

Edwards, R. (2018). *The eastern front: the Germans and Soviets at war in World War
    II.* Rowman & Littlefield.

8 things you need to know about the battle of Britain. (2018). Imperial War Museums.
    https://www.iwm.org.uk/history/8-things-you-need-to-know-about-
    the-battle-of-britain

Extermination camps. (2018). The Holocaust Explained: Designed for schools.
    https://www.theholocaustexplained.org/the-camps/types-of-
    camps/extermination-camps/

The extermination procedure in the gas chambers. (2022). Auschwitz-Birkenau State
    Museum. Www.auschwitz.org.
    https://www.auschwitz.org/en/history/auschwitz-and-shoah/the-
    extermination-procedure-in-the-gas-chambers/

"Final solution": overview. (2020, December 8). United States Holocaust
    Memorial Museum.
    https://encyclopedia.ushmm.org/content/en/article/final-solution-
    overview

Frischauer, W. (1964). *European commuter.* Macmillan.

Frost, N. (2020, January 21). *Horrors of Auschwitz: the numbers behind WWII's
    deadliest concentration camp.* HISTORY.
    https://www.history.com/news/auschwitz-concentration-camp-
    numbers

Gayle, T. (2018, August 8). *From hyperinflation to full employment: Nazi Germany's
    economic miracle explained.* History Hit.
    https://www.historyhit.com/nazi-germanys-economic-
    miracle/#:~:text=Before%20the%20Nazis%20took%20control

Gentry, C. (2021, March 22). *"Lady Death" of the Red Army: Lyudmila Pavlichenko.* The National WWII Museum New Orleans. https://www.nationalww2museum.org/war/articles/lady-death-red-army-lyudmila-pavlichenko

The German "lightning war" strategy of the second World War. (2018). Imperial War Museums. https://www.iwm.org.uk/history/the-german-lightning-war-strategy-of-the-second-world-war

German surrender. (n.d.). Encyclopedia.ushmm.org. https://encyclopedia.ushmm.org/content/en/timeline-event/holocaust/1942-1945/german-forces-surrender-to-the-allies

Germany surrenders. (n.d.). Anne Frank Website. https://www.annefrank.org/en/timeline/117/germany-surrenders/

Ghettos. (2019, December 4). United States Holocaust Memorial Museum. https://encyclopedia.ushmm.org/content/en/article/ghettos

Goldensohn, L. (2010). *The Nuremberg interviews: conversations with the defendants and witnesses.* Random House.

Goodman, P. (2014, October 6). *The 8 main reasons for war.* Owlcation. https://owlcation.com/social-sciences/The-Main-Reasons-For-War

Goodwin, D. (2001, December 19). *The way we won: America's economic breakthrough during World War II.* The American Prospect. https://prospect.org/health/way-won-america-s-economic-breakthrough-world-war-ii/

The great debate. (n.d.). The National WWII Museum New Orleans. https://www.nationalww2museum.org/war/articles/great-debate#:~:text=The%20Japanese%20attack%20on%20Pearl%20Harbor%20on%20December%207%2C%201941

Gruenbaum, O. (2017, January 21). *The Auschwitz survivor who returned to rescue her brother's paintings.* The Guardian. https://www.theguardian.com/lifeandstyle/2017/jan/21/eva-geiringer-schloss-auschwitz-holocaust-survivor-heinz-paintings

History.com Editors. (2009a). *Hitler descends into his bunker.* HISTORY. https://www.history.com/this-day-in-history/hitler-descends-into-his-bunker

History.com Editors. (2009b). *Marshall Plan*. HISTORY.
https://www.history.com/topics/world-war-ii/marshall-plan-1#impact-of-the-marshall-plan

History.com Editors (2009c). *Operation Barbarossa*. HISTORY.
https://www.history.com/topics/world-war-ii/operation-barbarossa#operation-barbarossa-begins

History.com Editors. (2009d, October 27). *Cold War history*. HISTORY.
https://www.history.com/topics/cold-war/cold-war-history

History.com Editors. (2009e, October 27). *D-Day*. HISTORY.
https://www.history.com/topics/world-war-ii/d-day#victory-in-normandy

History.com Editors. (2009f, November 18). *Bombing of Hiroshima and Nagasaki*. HISTORY. https://www.history.com/topics/world-war-ii/bombing-of-hiroshima-and-nagasaki#no-surrender-for-the-japanese

History.com Editors. (2018a, August 21). *Hirohito*. HISTORY.
https://www.history.com/topics/world-war-ii/hirohito-1

History.com Editors. (2018b, August 21). *Potsdam Conference*.
https://www.history.com/topics/world-war-ii/potsdam-conference

Holland, J. (2020, May 26). *9 things you (probably) didn't know about Dunkirk*.
HistoryExtra. https://www.historyextra.com/period/second-world-war/dunkirk-facts-history-east-mole-hitler-halt-order-douglas-jardine/

How Europe went to war in 1939. (n.d.). Imperial War Museums.
https://www.iwm.org.uk/history/how-europe-went-to-war-in-1939#:~:text=Germany%20represented%20a%20direct%20threat

How the Nazis lost WW2: Four major turning points. (n.d.). Sky HISTORY TV
Channel. https://www.history.co.uk/articles/how-the-nazis-lost-ww2-four-major-turning-points

Invasion of Poland, fall 1939. (2019, May 30). United States Holocaust Memorial
Museum.
https://encyclopedia.ushmm.org/content/en/article/invasion-of-poland-fall-1939

Irvine, A. (2021, January 18). *10 facts about Adolf Hitler's early life (1889-1919)*. History Hit. https://www.historyhit.com/facts-about-adolf-hitlers-early-life/

Irvine, A. (2023, January 13). *10 facts about Marshal Georgy Zhukov*. History Hit. https://www.historyhit.com/day-zhukov-takes-command-red-army-moscow/

Jacobs, F. (2023, February 6). *The horrors of World War II air war, in one stark map*. Big Think. https://bigthink.com/strange-maps/air-war-germany-map/#:~:text=The%20war%20had%20destroyed%204.8

Jakubek, A. M. (2019, September 30). *Teen diarist Renia Spiegel, "Poland's Anne Frank," gets her due after 80 years*. Times of Israel. https://www.timesofisrael.com/teen-diarist-renia-spiegel-polands-anne-frank-gets-her-due-after-80-years/

Jehovah's Witnesses. (n.d.). JW.ORG. https://www.jw.org/en/jehovahs-witnesses/faq/jw-holocaust-facts-concentration-camps/

Kearns, G. (2009). *Geopolitics and empire: the legacy of Halford Mackinder*. OUP Oxford.

Klein, C. (2020, August 11). *5 events that led to the end of World War II*. HISTORY. https://www.history.com/news/world-war-ii-end-events

Klein, C. (2019, April 26). *10 things you may not know about George Patton*. HISTORY. https://www.history.com/news/10-things-you-may-not-know-about-george-patton

Koenigsberg, R. A. (2007). *Hitler's ideology: embodied metaphor, fantasy and history*. IAP.

Lebovic, M. (2018, April 12). *The lost diary of Poland's "Anne Frank": An untold testament of a truncated life*. Times of Israel. https://www.timesofisrael.com/the-lost-diary-of-polands-anne-frank-an-untold-testament-of-a-truncated-life/

Lebrun, M. A. (2008). *Message addressed by M. Albert Lebrun, President of the Republic, to the French Parliament. September 2, 1939 (Chamber of Deputies. Sitting of Saturday, September 2, 1939 (Journal Officiel, of September 3, 1939*. Avalon.law.yale.edu.

https://avalon.law.yale.edu/wwii/ylbk355.asp#:~:text=Fortitude%2
C%20discipline%2C%20hopefulness%20have%20one

Letts, E. (2016). *The perfect horse: the daring U.S. mission to rescue the priceless stallions kidnapped by the Nazis.* Random House Publishing Group.

Liberation of Nazi camps. (2019). United States Holocaust Memorial Museum. https://encyclopedia.ushmm.org/content/en/article/liberation-of-nazi-camps

Ludwig, C. E. (2018). *But God...a journey.* Lulu.com.

Mady Gerrard. (2022, November 16). Bergen Belsen Concentration Camp. https://www.belsen.co.uk/mady-gerrard-survivor/

Maguire, S. (2019, January 21). *Want to find out how the World War II secret code was broken?* Donegal Daily. https://www.donegaldaily.com/2019/01/21/want-to-find-out-how-the-world-war-ii-secret-code-was-broken/

Mail Online. (2011, June 18). *Raped by the Russians... the harrowing secret of Mrs Helmut Kohl.* Daily Mail. https://www.dailymail.co.uk/news/article-2005343/Russian-soldiers-raped-wife-ex-German-chancellor-Helmut-Kohl-12.html

Martin, J. (2017, January 17). Lesser-known heroes of WWII. SBS What's On. https://www.sbs.com.au/whats-on/article/lesser-known-heroes-of-wwii/f8k7dfy8k

Mason, E. (2019, March 6). *The boys who lied about their age to fight in WW2.* HistoryExtra. https://www.historyextra.com/period/second-world-war/boys-who-lied-about-age-to-fight-ww2-teenage-soldiers/

Matthews, M. D. (2020). *Head strong: how psychology is revolutionizing war, revised and expanded edition.* Oxford University Press.

McLean, C. (2022, September 16). *When was World War II? The deadliest international conflict explained.* USA TODAY. https://www.usatoday.com/story/news/world/2022/09/16/when-was-world-war-2/8035788001/

McMenamin, M. (2018, November 8). *Meet the Irish spy who broke a Nazi cipher & changed WWII.* Spyscape.com.

https://spyscape.com/article/richard-hayes-the-irish-codebreaker-that-solved-the-nazi-gortz-cipher

Morson, G. S. (2011). *The words of others: from quotations to culture.* Yale University Press.

Mosaic of victims: in depth. (2019). United States Holocaust Memorial Museum. https://encyclopedia.ushmm.org/content/en/article/mosaic-of-victims-in-depth

Myre, G. (2019, April 18). *NPR choice page.* Npr.org. https://www.npr.org/2019/04/18/711356336/a-woman-of-no-importance-finally-gets-her-due

Nazi camps. (2009). United States Holocaust Memorial Museum. https://encyclopedia.ushmm.org/content/en/article/nazi-camps

Nazi Germany and fascist Italy become friends. (n.d.). Anne Frank House. https://www.annefrank.org/en/timeline/199/nazi-germany-and-fascist-italy-become-friends/#:~:text=In%20this%20treaty%2C%20the%20two

Nazi persecution: 1933–1945. (2023). Holocaust Memorial Day Trust. https://www.hmd.org.uk/learn-about-the-holocaust-and-genocides/nazi-persecution/

Neville Chamberlain quotes. (n.d.). BrainyQuote.com. https://www.brainyquote.com/quotes/neville_chamberlain_381690

Newborn, J. (2023, February 17). *Hans and Sophie Scholl were once Hitler youth leaders. why did they decide to stand up to the Nazis?* Smithsonian Magazine. https://www.smithsonianmag.com/history/hans-and-sophie-scholl-were-once-hitler-youth-leaders-why-did-they-decide-to-stand-up-to-the-nazis-180981643/

Nilsson, J. (2019, July 17). *If you were the average G.I. in World War II.* The Saturday Evening Post. https://www.saturdayeveningpost.com/2019/07/if-you-were-the-average-g-i-in-world-war-ii/

Norris, J. (2020). *Logistics in World War II: 1939–1945.* Pen and Sword Military.

Ouis, D. (2020). *Humorous wit.* Paragon Publishing.

Parkin, S. (2018, August 13). *5 major causes of World War Two in Europe*. History Hit. https://www.historyhit.com/causes-of-world-war-two-in-europe/

A Pearl Harbor fact sheet (pp. 1–2). (2001). The National WWII Museum. https://www.census.gov/history/pdf/pearl-harbor-fact-sheet-1.pdf

Political Prisoners. (2019). *United States Holocaust Memorial Museum*. https://encyclopedia.ushmm.org/content/en/article/political-prisoners

Pruitt, S. (2020, May 14). *The post World War II boom: how America got into gear*. History. https://www.history.com/news/post-world-war-ii-boom-economy

Reimann, M. (2016, October 7). *In one German town, 1,000 people killed themselves in 72 hours*. Medium. https://timeline.com/demmin-nazi-mass-suicide-44c6caf76727?gi=ef3e23450af1

Remembering resistance: Sophie Scholl and the white rose. (2022, February 23). Museum of Jewish Heritage. https://mjhnyc.org/blog/remembering-resistance-sophie-scholl-and-the-white-rose/

Research starters: worldwide deaths in World War II. (2022). The National WWII Museum New Orleans. https://www.nationalww2museum.org/students-teachers/student-resources/research-starters/research-starters-worldwide-deaths-world-war

RFE. (2018, February 2). *Russia marks 75th anniversary of Stalingrad victory*. RadioFreeEurope. https://www.rferl.org/a/battle-of-stalingrad-75th-anniversary-russia/29014053.html

Roos, D. (2019, June 5). *How many were killed on D-Day?* History. https://www.history.com/news/d-day-casualties-deaths-allies

Rosenberg, J. (2010, November 16). *Hitler's political statement*. ThoughtCo. https://www.thoughtco.com/hitlers-political-statement-1779643

6 little known facts about WWII. (n.d.). Sky HISTORY TV Channel. https://www.history.co.uk/articles/little-known-facts-about-wwii

Slater, L. (2018). *10 facts about the miracle of Dunkirk*. History Hit.
https://www.historyhit.com/facts-about-the-miracle-of-dunkirk/

Spiegel, R. (2018, October 24). *Hear, o Israel, save us* (A. Blasiak & M.
Dziurosz, Trans.). Smithsonian.
https://www.smithsonianmag.com/history/hear-o-israel-save-us-
renia-spiegel-diary-english-translation-holocaust-poland-180970536/

Spitzer, T. (2020, February 22). *Sophie Scholl and the white rose*. The National
WWII Museum New Orleans.
https://www.nationalww2museum.org/war/articles/sophie-scholl-
and-white-rose

Stan Scott. (n.d.). Gallery.commandoveterans.org.
https://gallery.commandoveterans.org/cdoGallery/v/units/3/Stan+
Scott/

Swinford, S. (2012). *Documents reveal Hitler's epic rant to senior Nazis 8 days before
he died*. Business Insider.
https://www.businessinsider.com/documents-reveal-hitlers-epic-
rant-to-senior-nazis-8-days-before-he-died-2012-10

Taylor, C. C. (2014). *8 attributes of great achievers*. Mount Lanai.

Team Mighty, We Are The Mighty. (2015, August 8). *21 rare and weird facts
about World War II*. Business Insider.
https://www.businessinsider.com/21-rare-and-weird-facts-about-
world-war-2-2015-8#12-the-siege-of-stalingrad-resulted-in-more-
russian-deaths-military-and-civilian-than-the-us-and-britain-sustained-
combined-in-all-of-world-war-ii-12

The Associated Press. (2023, April 9). *Ben Ferencz, the last living Nuremberg
prosecutor of Nazis, has died at 103*. NPR.
https://www.npr.org/2023/04/09/1168832384/ben-ferencz-last-
living-nuremberg-prosecutor-nazis-dies

Thomsett, M. C., & Thomsett, J. F. (2015). *War and conflict quotations: a
worldwide dictionary of pronouncements from military leaders, politicians,
philosophers, writers and others*. McFarland.

Tucker, P. (2013). *Secrets of acting Shakespeare: the original approach*. Routledge.

Ulam, A. (2018, February 12). *Why Renia Spiegel is being called "the Polish Anne Frank."* The Forward. https://forward.com/culture/394032/why-renia-spiegel-is-being-called-the-polish-anne-frank/

United States Holocaust Memorial Museum, Washington, DC. (2022, April 22). *Axis alliance in World War II.* Encyclopedia.ushmm.org. https://encyclopedia.ushmm.org/content/en/article/axis-powers-in-world-war-ii

United States Holocaust Memorial Museum. (2019). *The Soviet Union and the eastern front.* United States Holocaust Memorial Museum. https://encyclopedia.ushmm.org/content/en/article/the-soviet-union-and-the-eastern-front

Vogel, R. (2004). *Leadership and responsibility in the Second World War.* McGill-Queen's Press.

Warnock, B. (2020, January 24). *Nazis murdered a quarter of Europe's Roma, but history still overlooks this genocide.* The Conversation. https://theconversation.com/nazis-murdered-a-quarter-of-europes-roma-but-history-still-overlooks-this-genocide-128706

What you need to know about the battle of France. (n.d.). Imperial War Museums. https://www.iwm.org.uk/history/what-you-need-to-know-about-the-battle-of-france

Why did Hitler hate Jews? (2018, November 14). History on the Net. https://www.historyonthenet.com/why-did-hitler-hate-jews

Why did Japan join the Axis powers? (2022, April 24). Japan Luggage Express. https://www.jluggage.com/blog/history/why-did-japan-join-the-axis-powers/

Wiersbe, W. W. (1994). *Be available.* David C Cook.

Woerner, J. (2021, December 15). *Dunkirk evacuation and rescue during WWII.* Study.com. https://study.com/learn/lesson/dunkirk-evacuation-rescue.html#:~:text=How%20many%20died%20at%20Dunkirk

World War II (1939–1945): The invasion of France. (n.d.) SparkNotes. https://www.sparknotes.com/history/european/ww2/section2/

World War II for kids: after WWII post war. (2019). Ducksters.com.
https://www.ducksters.com/history/world_war_ii/after_ww2.php

World War II facts. (n.d.). FDR Presidential Library & Museum.
https://www.fdrlibrary.org/wwii-
facts#:~:text=In%20the%20aftermath%20of%20the

World War II for kids: technology. (2019). Ducksters.com.
https://www.ducksters.com/history/world_war_ii/technology_of_
ww2.php

Zuchowski, S. P. (2020, January 23). *12 quotes from survivors to read on
#HolocaustRemembranceDay.* Medium.
https://holocaustandhumanity.medium.com/12-quotes-from-
survivors-to-read-on-holocaustremembranceday-7db2dcf23910

Image References

Akg-images (1942) *Red Army / Stalingrad.* Alamy.
https://www.alamy.com/stock-photo-red-army-stalingrad-
september-1942-19377023.html

CBW (1940) *Fighter pilots "scramble" during the Battle of Britain, 1940.* Alamy.
https://www.alamy.com/fighter-pilots-scramble-during-the-battle-
of-britain-in-1940-image446405108.html

CBW (1944) *Jews from Subcarpathian Rus, then part of Hungary, await selection on the
ramp at Auschwitz II-Birkenau.* Alamy. https://www.alamy.com/jews-
from-subcarpathian-rus-then-part-of-hungary-await-selection-on-the-
ramp-at-auschwitz-ii-birkenau-selection-consisted-of-being-selected-
for-death-straight-away-in-the-gas-chambers-or-being-sent-as-a-
forced-slave-labourer-image544

Chronicle (c. 1943) *Munitions produced by the inmates of Dachau Concentration Camp
for the Nazi war effort.* Alamy. https://www.alamy.com/stock-photo-
munitions-produced-by-the-inmates-of-dachau-concentration-camp-
for-105317376.html

Cola Images (c. 1940-43) *Wall of the Warsaw Ghetto.* Alamy.
https://www.alamy.com/stock-photo-the-wall-of-the-warsaw-
ghetto-poland-89273321.html

Dave Bagnall Collection (1940) *Chaos on the streets of Macon, France in June 1940 during the Battle of France.* Alamy. https://www.alamy.com/stock-photo-chaos-on-the-streets-of-macon-france-in-june-1940-during-the-battle-175344792.html

David Cole (1942) *Joseph Stalin, Premier of the Soviet Union from 6 May 1941 until his death in 5 March 1953.* Alamy. https://www.alamy.com/stock-photo-joseph-vissarionovich-stalin-was-the-premier-of-the-soviet-union-from-97973229.html

DPA picture alliance (1943) *Brother and sister Hans and Sophie Scholl, members of the White Rose, a non-violent resistance movement in Nazi Germany.* Alamy. https://www.alamy.com/the-scholl-siblings-refers-to-brother-and-sister-hans-and-sophie-scholl-who-were-members-of-the-white-rose-a-non-violent-resistance-movement-in-nazi-germany-today-there-are-many-streets-and-schools-in-germany-named-for-the-scholl-siblings-there-is-also-a-literary-prize-in-their-honor-the-geschwister-scholl-preis-usage-worldwide-image243758540.html

Good Free Photos (1945) *Allied military personnel in Paris celebrating V-J Day, End of World War II* https://www.goodfreephotos.com/historical-battles/world-war-ii/allied-military-personnel-in-paris-celebrating-v-j-day-end-of-world-war-ii.jpg.php

Good Free Photos (1944) *American troops approaching Omaha Beach on Normandy Beach, D-Day* https://www.goodfreephotos.com/historical-battles/world-war-ii/american-troops-approaching-omaha-beach-on-normandy-beach-d-day-world-war-ii.jpg.php

Good Free Photos (1944) *British Sherman Tank, the Firefly at the Battle of the Bulge, World War II.* https://www.goodfreephotos.com/albums/historical-battles/world-war-ii/british-sherman-tank-firefly-battle-of-the-bulge-world-war-ii.jpg

Good Free Photos (1945) *A devastated street in the city centre just off the Unter den Linden after Battle of Berlin* https://www.goodfreephotos.com/historical-battles/world-war-ii/a-devastated-street-in-the-city-centre-just-off-the-unter-den-linden-after-battle-of-berlin.jpg.php

Good Free Photos (1942) *Devastators on the USS Enterprise in Battle of Midway* https://www.goodfreephotos.com/historical-battles/world-war-ii/devastators-on-the-uss-enterprise-in-world-war-ii-battle-of-midway.jpg.php

Good Free Photos (1945) *Field Marshall Wilhelm Keitel signs the final surrender terms, Victory in Europe* https://www.goodfreephotos.com/historical-battles/world-war-ii/field-marshall-willhelm-keitel-signs-the-final-surrender-terms-victory-in-europe.jpg.php

Good Free Photos (1940) *German Luftwaffe, Heinkel He 111 bombers during the Battle of Britain in World War II.* https://www.goodfreephotos.com/albums/historical-battles/world-war-ii/german-luftwaffe-heinkel-he-111-bombers-during-battle-of-britain-world-war-ii.jpg

Good Free Photos (1944) *German machine gunner marching through the Ardennes in the Battle of the Bulge* https://www.goodfreephotos.com/albums/historical-battles/world-war-ii/german-machine-gunner-marching-through-the-ardennes-in-the-battle-of-the-bulge.jpg

Good Free Photos (1942) *Japanese cruiser Mikuma shortly before sinking during Battle of Midway.* https://www.goodfreephotos.com/historical-battles/world-war-ii/mikuma-shortly-before-sinking-battle-of-midway-world-war-ii.jpg.php

Good Free Photos (1945) *Winston Churchill Waves to Crowd After V-E Day, End of War in Europe* https://www.goodfreephotos.com/albums/historical-battles/world-war-ii/winston-churchill-waves-to-crowd-after-v-e-day-end-of-war-in-europe.jpg

Granger, Historical Picture Archive (1938) *Benito Mussolini, Italian Leader, photographed 1938.* Alamy. https://www.alamy.com/stock-photo-benito-mussolini-1883-1945-nitalian-political-leader-photographed-95407058.html

Heritage Images (1945) *Vintage photo of General George Patton.* Alamy. https://www.alamy.com/stock-photo-vintage-photo-of-general-george-patton-49091068.html

Ian Dagnall Computing (1933) *Franklin D Roosevelt (1882-1945), portrait of the 32nd President of the USA, c. Dec 1933.* Alamy.

https://www.alamy.com/stock-photo-franklin-d-roosevelt-1882-1945-portrait-of-the-32nd-president-of-the-123238911.html

Ian Dagnall Computing (1944) Georgy Zhukov *(1896-1974), 1944*. Alamy. https://www.alamy.com/georgy-zhukov-portrait-of-the-soviet-general-georgy-konstantinovich-zhukov-1896-1974-1944-image426526295.html

Interfoto (1933) *Nazism, persecution of the Jews, boycott of Jewish stores, storm battalion man and SS man sticking boycott poster on shop window, "Deutsche! Wehrt Euch! Kauft nicht bei Juden!" probably Berlin, Germany, 1.4.1933.* Alamy. https://www.alamy.com/nazism-national-socialism-persecution-of-the-jews-boycott-of-jewish-stores-storm-battalion-man-and-ss-man-sticking-boycott-poster-on-shop-window-deutsche!-wehrt-euch!-kauft-nicht-bei-juden!-probably-berlin-germany-141933-additional-rights-clearance-info-not-available-image240732101.html

Niday Picture Library (1940) *Soldiers from the British Expeditionary Force fire at low flying German aircraft during the Dunkirk evacuation.* Alamy. https://www.alamy.com/soldiers-from-the-british-expeditionary-force-fire-at-low-flying-german-aircraft-during-the-dunkirk-evacuation-june-1940-image352972913.html

Photo 12 (1946) *Nuremberg trial (1945-1946), the accused.* Alamy. https://www.alamy.com/stock-photo-nuremberg-trial-1945-1946-the-accused-49985515.html

Pictorial Press Ltd (1940) *Adolf Hitler (1889-1945) giving the Nazi salute from his Mercedes-Benz in Berlin in July 1940 after his visit to German-occupied Paris.* Alamy. https://www.alamy.com/adolf-hitler-1889-1945-giving-the-nazi-salute-from-his-mercedes-benz-in-berlin-in-july-1940-after-his-visit-to-german-occupied-paris-note-camerman-at-left-image462841133.html

Shawshots (1941) *A column of Nazi Germany armoured forces, including PzKpfw III Ausf G tanks on Eastern Moscow front. 1941 Soviet Russia Operation Barbarossa, original name Operation Fritz, during World War II, code name for the German invasion of the Soviet Union, which was launched on June 22, 1941.* Alamy.https://www.alamy.com/operation-barbarossa-ww2-a-column-of-nazi-germany-armoured-forces-including-pzkpfw-iii-ausf-g-tanks-on-a-forest-road-on-the-eastern-moscow-front-1941-soviet-russia-operation-barbarossa-original-name-operation-fritz-during-world-war-ii-code-name-for-the-german-invasion-of-the-soviet-union-which-was-launched-on-june-22-1941-the-failure-of-german-troops-to-defeat-soviet-russian-forces-in-the-campaign-signaled-a-crucial-turning-point-in-the-war-image456375365.html

Shawshots (1940) *Formation of Hawker Hurricanes of RAF Fighter Command, on patrol defending against Nazi Germany bombers, 1940.* Alamy. https://www.alamy.com/hawker-hurricane-aircraft-1940-vintage-ww2-battle-of-britain-squadron-formation-of-hawker-hurricanes-of-raf-fighter-command-on-patrol-defending-against-nazi-germany-bombers-indiscriminately-attacking-general-populated-areas-in-britain-during-the-blitz-of-1940-image231850602.html

Shawshots (1942) *Jewish women & children some wearing Nazi designated yellow stars arrive by cattle rail trucks to Auschwitz-Birkenau, a WW2 German Nazi Concentration camp.* Alamy. https://www.alamy.com/auschwitz-birkenau-arrivals-jewish-women-children-some-wearing-nazi-designated-yellow-stars-arrive-by-cattle-rail-trucks-to-auschwitz-birkenau-a-ww2-german-nazi-concentration-camp-jewish-children-were-the-largest-group-deported-to-the-camp-they-were-sent-along-with-adults-beginning-in-early-1942-as-part-of-final-solution-of-the-jewish-questionthe-total-destruction-of-the-jewish-population-of-europeauschwitz-concentration-camp-was-a-network-of-german-nazi-concentration-and-extermination-camps-operated-by-the-third-reich-in-polish-areas-annexed-by-nazi-germany-during-world-war-ii-image349860151.html

Shawshots (1945) *Russian soldier raising Soviet Hammer and Sickle flag over the Nazi Reichstag chancellery taken during the Battle of Berlin.* Alamy. https://www.alamy.com/russian-flag-berlin-1945-reichstag-iconic-world-war-2-germany-russian-soldier-raising-soviet-hammer-and-sickle-flag-over-the-nazi-reichstag-chancellory-a-historic-world-war-ii-photograph-taken-during-the-battle-of-berlin-on-2-may-1945-it-shows-meliton-kantaria-and-mikhail-yegorov-raising-the-soviet-flag-over-the-former-nazi-germany-seat-of-power-the-berlin-reichstag-berlin-germany-archive-image-digitally-restored-and-processed-to-its-original-impact-and-quality-potential-image208042352.html

Shawshots (1940) *WW2 German medium tank PzKpfw IV with tactical number 625 of 12. SS-Panzer-Division "Hitlerjugend" during the Battle of France.* Alamy. https://www.alamy.com/ww2-german-medium-tank-pzkpfw-iv-with-tactical-number-625-of-12-ss-panzer-division-hitlerjugend-during-the-battle-of-france-western-front-world-war-ii-the-battle-of-france-10-may-25-june-1940-also-known-as-the-western-campaign-the-fr

Sueddeutsche Zeitung Photo (1940) *BEF soldiers from France arrive in southern England aboard a destroyer.* Alamy. https://www.alamy.com/bef-soldiers-from-france-arrive-in-southern-england-aboard-a-destroyer-image247157269.html

Sueddeutsche Zeitung Photo (1938) *A burning synagogue during Kristallnacht, Baden-Baden, 9th November 1938.* Alamy. https://www.alamy.com/a-burning-synagogue-during-kristallnacht-baden-baden-9th-november-1938-bw-photo-image247136532.html

Sueddeutsche Zeitung Photo (1942) *Nazi German machine gunner in Stalingrad.* Alamy. https://www.alamy.com/stock-photo-nazi-german-machine-gunner-in-stalingrad-1942-36991375.html

US National Archives (1940) *Adolf Hitler and Benito Mussolini in Munich, Germany 1940* https://catalog.archives.gov/id/540151

US National Archives (1939) *German troops parade before Hitler in Warsaw after the invasion of Poland.* https://catalog.archives.gov/id/175539501

US National Archives (n.d.) *Hitler speaks at Party Rally.* National Archives Catalog: https://catalog.archives.gov/id/162124785

US National Archives (1941) *Japanese attack on Pearl Harbor, Hawaii.* https://catalog.archives.gov/id/197288

US National Archives (n.d.) *Portrait of Adolf Hitler.* https://catalog.archives.gov/id/162121492

US National Archives (c.1942) *Portrait of Emperor Hirohito* https://catalog.archives.gov/id/213259750

US National Archives (1945) *Virginia Hall of Special Operations Branch receiving the Distinguished Service Cross* https://catalog.archives.gov/id/595150

World History Archive (1944) *The D-Day invasion of Normandy, 1944.* Alamy. https://www.alamy.com/stock-photo-june-1944-the-d-day-invasion-of-normandy-80458448.html

World History Archive (1940) *The evacuation of the British troops. Dunkirk.* Alamy. https://www.alamy.com/the-evacuation-of-the-british-troops-dunkirk-1940-image481949104.html

World History Archive (1943) *Winston Churchill (1874-1965) British politician who was the Prime Minister of the United Kingdom.* Alamy. https://www.alamy.com/stock-photo-photograph-of-winston-churchill-1874-1965-british-politician-who-was-90828988.html